AWAKENING THE
LUMINOUS MIND

Also by Tenzin Wangyal Rinpoche

*Awakening the Sacred Body**

Healing with Form, Energy, and Light

Tibetan Sound Healing

Tibetan Yogas of Body, Speech, and Mind

The Tibetan Yogas of Dream and Sleep

Unbounded Wholeness (with Anne Klein)

Wonders of the Natural Mind

*Available from Hay House

Please visit:

Hay House USA: **www.hayhouse.com**®
Hay House Australia: **www.hayhouse.com.au**
Hay House UK: **www.hayhouse.co.uk**
Hay House South Africa: **www.hayhouse.co.za**
Hay House India: **www.hayhouse.co.in**

AWAKENING THE
LUMINOUS MIND

Tibetan Meditation for Inner Peace and Joy

TENZIN WANGYAL RINPOCHE

EDITED BY MARCY VAUGHN

HAY HOUSE, INC.
Carlsbad, California • New York City
London • Sydney • Johannesburg
Vancouver • Hong Kong • New Delhi

Published and distributed in the United States by: Hay House, Inc.: www.hayhouse
.com® • *Published and distributed in Australia by:* Hay House Australia Pty. Ltd.:
www.hayhouse.com.au • *Published and distributed in the United Kingdom by:*
Hay House UK, Ltd.: www.hayhouse.co.uk • *Published and distributed in the
Republic of South Africa by:* Hay House SA (Pty), Ltd.: www.hayhouse.co.za •
Distributed in Canada by: Raincoast: www.raincoast.com • *Published in India
by:* Hay House Publishers India: www.hayhouse.co.in

Cover design: Tricia Breidenthal • *Interior design:* Pamela Homan

Library of Congress Cataloging-in-Publication Data

Wangyal, Tenzin.
  Awakening the luminous mind : Tibetan meditation for inner peace and
joy / Tenzin Wangyal Rinpoche ; edited by Marcy Vaughn. -- 1st edition.
     pages cm
  ISBN 978-1-4019-3761-4 (pbk.)
  1. Meditation--Bon (Tibetan religion) I. Vaughn, Marcy, editor. II.
Title.
  BQ7982.2.W326 2012
  299.5'4--dc23
                                        2012010774

Tradepaper ISBN: 978-1-4019-3761-4
Digital ISBN: 978-1-4019-3762-1

15 14 13 12   4 3 2 1
1st edition, June 2012

FSC
www.fsc.org

MIX

Paper from
responsible sources

FSC® C011935

Printed in the United States of America

CONTENTS

PREFACE

Meditation is a method of recognizing and being aware of the inherent completeness of each moment. It is not a matter of cultivating or finding something you don't have, but of being aware of what you already have. The awareness of one's inherent completeness is pure, and this awareness pervades all that is experienced, and guides all of our actions. The methods in this book do not involve learning rituals or following complicated philosophies. Rather, you are pointed to experience life directly, without any religious or philosophical views, forms, or divisions.

Among the practices we will directly experience in the book are the meditation instructions of Dawa Gyaltsen, a Tibetan Bön *dzogchen* master who lived in the 8th century. Dawa Gyaltsen was the 24th *dzogchen* master of my lineage, called the Zhang Zhung Nyen Gyü, or oral tradition of Zhang Zhung, in which spoken instructions were passed down from teacher to student over the centuries in the ancient land of Zhang Zhung, and then Tibet. The Tibetan name of his teachings, *dzogchen*, means great perfection or great completeness. At the core of *dzogchen* is the view that all sentient beings are primordially pure and perfected, with the potential to spontaneously manifest in a beneficial way. This traditional language may sound mysterious, but it simply means that from its very origin, our nature is perfectly pure and complete; and this purity, when it is unobstructed, can express itself effortlessly, in a way that benefits everyone. This capacity is within each and every one of us. It is our nature. When we fail to recognize this true nature, we suffer and can cause harm to others. When we do recognize our inherent nature, we are able to liberate our own suffering. As we mature in this recognition, we can be of great comfort and help to others.

Many of the *dzogchen* masters were not intellectuals or scholars. Some couldn't even read. But the transmission of the teachings from master to student, and the warmth and blessing of this connection, remain unbroken to this day. Traditionally, the teacher introduced the student to the nature of mind, which is already pure and complete. He or she "pointed out" or affirmed a recognition that the student was having. After receiving these pointing-out instructions, the students meditated in solitude for a period of time until their meditative realization became stable. Their realization would then be expressed in a few lines of spiritual advice directly from the heart. They imparted this heart advice, the fruit of their practice, to the next student, who in turn contemplated and practiced it until also attaining realization. Dawa Gyaltsen's heart instructions consist of five lines, referred to as the Fivefold Teaching of Dawa Gyaltsen. These lines constitute a simple, elegant, and complete path to realization.

Vision is mind.
Mind is empty.
Emptiness is clear light.
Clear light is union.
Union is great bliss.

These five lines describe a path of pure awareness, leading us from confusion to great bliss. They are applicable in any situation and in any moment. As a young monk, I carried these five lines in my pocket when I left my birthplace, India, for the first time, having been called to teach the Tibetan Bön tradition to the West. I would often sit in an Italian café and contemplate the lines as I observed life streaming around me. Now in the United States, they continue to guide me in my life as husband, father, and teacher.

As you learn the meaning of the five lines of advice and begin to meditate on them, you will be encouraged to look directly and intimately within, and discover the jewel that is hidden in your ordinary experiences. Very often, we look outside of ourselves for help, advice, or relief, rejecting our own experience because we may not know how to work with it. Often we are filled with self-doubt and self-judgment. On any journey, it is important to know where to turn when we feel disconnected or confused in this way. That is why the principle of refuge is most essential—knowing how to turn within when we need help. Thus, I will devote Chapters 1 through 3 to the discovery of inner refuge.

I will also share with you a teaching poem of inner refuge that I wrote as a form of guidance for my students. It will encourage you to honor and respect the "three doors" of your body, speech, and mind as opportunities for healing, and I hope it will inspire you to discover your inherent positive qualities. The poem appears in Chapter 2 and the appendix, and is also recited on the CD.

Once you have discovered the inner refuge, in Chapters 4 through 8 you will explore each of the five lines of heart advice given by Dawa Gyaltsen, learning how to contemplate them with guided meditation practices. As you connect with the openness, awareness, and warmth of being who you truly are, you will be connecting with the blessings of the practitioners and masters who have gone before you, for they connected to themselves through meditation just as you are doing today.

To engage these teachings, you need not adopt or rely upon a particular faith or belief; you need only be willing to face the experiences of your life directly and nakedly. The idea is to integrate the teachings with your life as you are living it. No matter what position you hold in life, or what particular stage of life you are in, wherever you are, I offer these teachings with the hope that you gain realization, transforming your perceived limitations into gifts. This is my prayer. And no matter what you do in life, if your actions are connected to the open source of being that is within you, the outcome will be beneficial, for it is only when we lose connection to the source of wisdom and light within ourselves that we suffer and cause harm to others.

May you discover the treasury of your natural mind and receive the many benefits available to enrich your life. May you experience the blessings of the lineage, which support deep personal healing, as you allow the teachings of Dawa Gyaltsen to enter your heart. May the fruit of your practice ripen and offer nourishment to you and to countless others.

Tenzin Wangyal Rinpoche
October 2011

INTRODUCTION

The path of meditation presented in this book is not a matter of merely learning techniques and concepts. After all, we are lively, warmhearted beings, not mechanical objects. Therefore, to evolve and mature as feeling beings, we need a sense of where to turn when we become confused or encounter difficulties. In my tradition, we obtain this help by going for *inner refuge*. Seeking refuge is not a vague abstraction, nor is it a plea for help. It involves helping ourselves by focusing our attention in very specific ways. When we do this, the discoveries that we make and the benefits that become available are clearly discernible.

What do we commonly do whenever we feel confused? We reject our confusion and try to get rid of it or push it away; we magnify it by dwelling upon it and becoming lost in it; or we disconnect from our confusion by distracting ourselves. Typically, we look outside ourselves for some kind of comfort, support, or advice. However, it is not possible to find what we truly seek by looking outward. We may think we have found something out there, but it is temporary, and in the end we lose what we have found, or we constantly worry about losing it. Ultimately, any external support is not the best medicine for our suffering. To find the best medicine, we must turn within. Turning within doesn't imply improving our ideas, challenging our thoughts, or changing our feelings. It means turning inside to find support in what we already are.

When you are stressed or challenged, bring your attention inward. Usually your attention is not directed inward; it is fixated on whatever is challenging you. You think thoughts such as *My health is not good. . . . I am worried about this change. . . . That person is annoying me.* Your attention is separated from yourself and focused on "the problem," which could be a person or a situation. And your thoughts go back and forth, trying to solve this problem or complaining about that situation or person. Maybe you divert your attention altogether and dwell on something else because your problem is too overwhelming. Or you accommodate yourself to the situation, thinking that acceptance is sane or noble or mature. In all these ways, no matter how creative or sophisticated they are, you are reinforcing your identity as the one who suffers. I call this a pain identity. No matter how familiar any pain identity may be, this is not who you truly are.

Inner refuge is the recognition of your true nature, which, according to these teachings, is the open and clear space of being. This is the nature of your true identity: open and clear. This nature is often referred to as the natural mind. It can be directly perceived, but not by the moving, problem-solving mind; only pure awareness can apprehend it. The awareness of openness is the source of all healing as well as the source of creativity, joy, love, compassion, and all other positive qualities.

To discover this source within, this inner refuge, you must shift your focus or attention from the perception of a problem to the awareness of *being* itself. This book provides specific guidance on how to do this, on how to recognize what is true in the midst of confusion. It will guide you to bring awareness to the ordinary experiences of everyday life, for these experiences, which may appear bounded and limited, can become doorways to experiencing the magic of infinite possibilities. It is not a matter of the technique of this meditation or that meditation, although there are many useful and skillful techniques to help you. More than any technique, what is important is your relation to yourself. Changing your life is a matter of connecting with places in yourself you may have never fully connected with, and understanding things you may never have fully understood or trusted. Do you recognize and honor the *space of being*, the truth of who you are, in the life in which you find yourself? This space within yourself is not a passive place where nothing happens. The whole universe arises, rests, and dissolves in that single space. Everything in your body arises, rests, and dissolves in that space. Surely we can trust that there is a deeper intelligence at work than the intelligence of ego with all its plans and proposals. Solutions will come naturally from the connection with the open space of being, which is boundless and infinitely full of potential.

If you follow the principles in this book, guidance, creativity, and intelligence will naturally and spontaneously arise as you recognize and connect with the openness of being fully present. You will see changes happening in your everyday life. Trust that openness is the source. Discovering this is not a passive experience; it is lively and participatory. As you come to know the liveliness of connecting to the infinite possibilities of each moment, you will experience an inherent sense of worthiness and richness. Your actions will spontaneously arise from the warmth of connection and will bring benefits and blessings to yourself and others.

Using This Book and CD

In the following chapters, I will describe a series of meditations designed so that you might practice along with them. After reading each chapter, you may wish to pause, listen to, and practice along with the corresponding track on the CD. This will help you to become more familiar with each practice and to bring what you have been reading and reflecting upon directly into your experience in a deeper way. This is the traditional Buddhist way of progressing on the path: reading or hearing the teaching, reflecting upon what you have read or heard, and then bringing what you have understood directly into your meditation practice.

You may wish to use the CD frequently as a support for your meditation practice. I recommend beginning a session of practice with the refuge poem. Engaging the inner refuge as guided on the CD will establish a foundation for your practice and can be a complete practice in itself. If you continue on, you may choose one or all of the tracks corresponding to the lines of Dawa Gyaltsen to reflect upon. Your practice finds completion as you bring the fruits of your meditation practice into everyday life. It is traditional to conclude a period of meditation, no matter how brief, with the intention to dedicate the merit of one's practice for the benefit of others. A traditional dedication poem is provided in both Tibetan and English as a support to express such an intention. You will also find a copy of this poem in English in the appendix.

CHAPTER ONE

FINDING REFUGE THROUGH THE THREE DOORS

Our ordinary experience offers us three opportunities to transform our lives and find the inner peace, joy, and liberation from suffering that we all wish for. Since our confusion is expressed through our body, our speech, and our mind, these three places also offer opportunities to dispel that confusion. The three areas of body, speech, and mind are referred to as the three doors. By shifting our attention in specific ways—away from the expression of pain and toward the release of that pain—we enter these doorways to discover the gifts of openness, awareness, and warmth.

There are three ways in which you will learn to shift attention. While directing attention to the pain body, you are instructed to feel the *stillness* of the body. While directing attention to pain speech, you connect with hearing the *silence*. And while you direct your attention to the pain mind, or the moving mind, the instruction is to recognize and connect with *spaciousness*. In these ways, it is possible to find a deep place of stillness, silence, and spaciousness. These three doorways lead to accessing important places of protection and refuge.

Many people find it difficult to become aware of the space of *being* itself rather than simply being aware of the sensations they are feeling, the inner dialogue they are having, or the contents of the moving mind altogether. What kind of shift are we describing? First, it is necessary to open and simply experience your discomfort. Can you be fully open, as the sky is with the clouds? In this analogy, clouds can refer to your thoughts, feelings, sensations, or memories. Does the sky have a problem with the clouds? Is the sky agitated? Does the sky say, "You have been here too long! Why are you still here? What does it mean that you are here?" No. The sky simply allows the presence of clouds, and when the clouds eventually dissipate, the sky does not comment. The sky is not lonely when the clouds leave. Can you *be* like that sky and host the clouds? If you are able to do that—to be with your pain directly—the pain heals itself: it self-liberates. As your pain or discomfort shifts, it is important to simply remain present and aware of the openness itself.

Each person's path is unique, and each must be willing to directly experience the sense of limitation and pain as it occurs in body, speech, and mind, and become familiar with turning to the inner refuge to discover the positive benefits that arise in so doing. It is important to recognize that we pay so much attention to ego, to our problem-solving, moving mind. We must recognize ego for what it is—a pain identity. We have a constant dialogue of pain talking to pain, which is what usually guides us or drives us, sometimes driving us crazy. And no matter how smart or sophisticated, ego only operates within the logic of pain, and therefore produces more pain. Perhaps it is time to discover there is something other than ego to turn toward and to trust.

For each of us to heal personal, family, and societal suffering, we need to recognize the habitual reactions that obscure our true nature and block us from living in full relation to our inherent intelligence and capacity. Our habitual reactions to the challenges in life I refer to as the *pain body*. By using the word *body*, I am not only referring to the physical body with its tensions, aches, constrictions, and illnesses, but to our sense of identity altogether, our sense of "I" or "me." In the Bön teachings, this identity is known as the "karmic conceptual pain body." This pain body is who you feel and think you are in any given moment.

It is useful to draw your attention to moments of pain and challenge in your life because the pain body is more obvious in those moments. When we react in stressful moments, the karmic conceptual pain body is triggered. But this sense of "me," this "I," is a completely false idea of self. Perhaps you have heard yourself saying at one time or another, "I'm going through a hard time. I broke up with my wife. I'm having a hard time with my boss. I am getting old. I am sick." I. I. I. Who is that "I"? Is it really you? It appears to be so. That's what you believe, and in a particularly painful moment, you may have full conviction in that identity. And yet it is your belief in your identity that is the fundamental problem.

From this sense of "I" develops pain speech, which articulates the distress of separation. Sometimes this distress can be felt as restless, upward-moving sensations in the chest, throat, and breath, and often it emerges outwardly in speech, or inwardly as inner dialogue. It can be as simple as a sigh or as elaborate as habitual negative self-talk that accompanies us through our sleeping and waking hours, often unrecognized for the damage it does in reinforcing our pain identity.

As human beings we are storytellers. The pain mind involves the imagination of ego, the story that is woven of thoughts and images that may appear intelligent, but fail to recognize the truth of the fundamental separation from our essential nature. Our stories can delight and amuse as well as shock and horrify us. But we are not our stories. And no matter how smart or sophisticated the storyteller is, the pain mind cannot liberate us from the suffering we experience.

What *does* liberate suffering? The moment you have some glimpse that you are bigger than what you are thinking or feeling is a healing moment. In such a moment, the false sense of "I" begins to lose its grip. Through meditation, noticing this dissolution of a solid self is encouraged by drawing your attention to the sense of being itself, rather than to a given momentary reaction. The moment that false sense of "I" starts to dissipate, you begin to feel different. If you trust in the space that opens up, you can discover a deeper support than the reactivity of your ego. This deeper support is the inner refuge, and this is your protection.

Our false self thinks, *This is not okay. That person has hurt me so much. This is not acceptable to me.* Or, *I have to push back. I have to be strategic. I need the upper hand.* Who is that "me," that "I"? We want to have a very clear sense of being a victim or a victor. But that view, that ego, those voices, are what we need protection from, because from this "I" we suffer. How do you connect with what is larger than "I"? You don't connect with what is larger than "I" by having a conversation with that "I." You don't connect by negotiating with "I." You don't try to improve it, destroy it, or ignore it either. You start by simply feeling what you are feeling. The very moment in which you feel awkwardness, confusion, irritation, or a reaction of any kind is an opportunity to discover that you are not that reaction.

To take full advantage of the challenges in our life so that they become the doorways to healing and positive development, we need to discover where to look. Go to stillness, go to silence, go to spaciousness. From these three places, allow your reaction.

You allow it by not resisting, talking back, or rejecting it in any way. And, at the same time, you are not allowing it to affect your stillness, your silence, your spaciousness. If you examine your own experience, you will often find that, because of fear, you do not allow pain to be as simple as it is in the moment. And because we fear pain and vulnerability, we try to manage it, to handle it. I refer to the one who is managing and handling the situation as "the smart ego." While it may seem reassuring to have some aspect of ourselves in charge of a given situation, the smart ego is not the one who will find release from that false identity and find the end to suffering. You think that smart voice is the solution. That is a mistaken belief. Because it is so easy to believe in the false ego, it is all the more important to find inner refuge in stillness, silence, and spaciousness.

The teachings of Bön *dzogchen*, as mentioned in the preface, tell us that our natural mind is pure and perfected, giving rise spontaneously to positive qualities such as love, joy, compassion, and equanimity. We do not need to directly cultivate these positive qualities nor produce them through effort, because they naturally arise. That is why *recognizing* the natural mind is the inner refuge, and is the purpose of the meditation practices in this book. We access the inner refuge through the experience of the stillness of the body, silence of speech, and spaciousness of mind, the three doors.

The inner refuge of the natural mind is not a belief or a concept. This experience has no shape, no color, no definition, no single location, nor is it the product of any religion or philosophy. Recognizing the natural mind, we are freed from suffering; failing to recognize this, we continue to suffer. The discovery of the natural mind heals divisions, resolves conflicting emotions and thoughts, and extinguishes confusion and suffering. When we recognize our natural mind, and attain stability and maturity in the recognition of this source within, we refer to this attainment as enlightenment. As humans, we each have an incredible treasure, a place of wisdom in ourselves. But we have lost touch with the refuge within ourselves.

FINDING INNER REFUGE THROUGH THE STILLNESS OF THE BODY

How do you find inner refuge through the door of the body? How can you find that place of stillness in yourself when you feel agitated or disturbed? First, don't move your body. Let it settle. Allow your pain to breathe. Second, don't feed your body negative attention or worry; it is important to draw the right kind of attention to the body. Become still and focus your attention upon stillness. That's your door. Go deeper toward this stillness. It is possible that in ten minutes you'll arrive at a deep place in yourself. When you come to a place of stillness, there is a natural sense of expansion or spaciousness. This sense of being, this spaciousness that you experience is indestructible. You don't take refuge in something that can be destroyed or changed. You take refuge in something that does not change. That refuge is the spaciousness of being. Even if you only glimpse it, that glimpse is enough to begin to trust. Trusting the place of inner refuge is very important. Once you arrive in the place of deep stillness, you feel a complete sense of protection. So in this way, the body is one door to inner refuge.

Sometimes we lose touch with our essence and get caught up in how we look or feel and what we possess. Of course, the body is important and needs to be taken care of, because it is a door to experiencing your essence. The body gives access to deep stillness, which allows you to experience wisdom. Ultimately, we are able to experience inner stillness as the subtle flow of awareness in the body. The purpose of Tibetan yoga is to support the subtle movement of this awareness. (For more information on Tibetan yoga, see my book *Awakening the Sacred Body*, Hay House 2011.)

When we are conscious through and within our body, we find that inner body. You might call it a *sacred body*. This is the awakening of the sacred body. You have an experience of ground or being or self beyond what you feel with the ordinary body and its changeable conditions. You have a sense of being that is beyond ignorance and the dualistic fears of the ego. You can go beyond all that by connecting to this deep place in a very simple way—by connecting through stillness. It is not complicated. If you experience it, it is the most exciting thing you can do. When you face an incredible challenge or experience pain, and in a second can shift to a place of total peace, it's a very powerful experience. It's valuable and absolutely necessary. That is how we find protection—by finding refuge through the stillness of the body.

FINDING INNER REFUGE THROUGH THE SILENCE OF SPEECH

How do you find inner refuge through the door of speech? The pain body has its own speech. It has its own voices. It's not hard to avoid certain people, change your job, and get a divorce, but it's very difficult to get divorced from your inner critical voices. Even if you go on a beautiful holiday, pain speech travels with you. If you go to the beach, it's there. If you go to the mountains for fresh air, the inner dialogue is still running. How is it possible to overcome your inner critic? It is not possible by more talking, not even by more "intelligent" talking, which is what we commonly try.

You may say, "I don't have problems with debt; I just don't think about it. I'm busy with my work, and I have an active social life." But when you are awake at three in the morning, you begin to think about your debt. Is that a good time to do this? No. But there you are, in your bed, unable to get back to sleep because you're having a conversation with yourself. It's very noisy. So you negotiate with your inner voices and come to a temporary intellectual peace. You find reasons to be calm. You find reasons to feel good. If you want to produce reasons to be calm and peaceful, you can. But that is not the solution for your unrest, because no matter how intelligently you reason, it is part of pain speech.

So what can you do? Focus your attention and listen to the silence. If your voices are persistent, simply allow the voices and feel the space and the silence around them, instead of listening to them and trying to negotiate with them. Feel the silence in and around the voices rather than trying to find the silence in the absence of voices. You don't need to run away from noise to find silence. You find the silence within the noise. Begin to hear the silence. It is there. It has always been there. You can discover it. Basically you are neither rejecting your inner voices nor inviting them. You're just being completely open. Openness is the key. As the sky hosts the clouds, silence hosts all sounds, whether external or internal.

A man I knew bought a house on a beautiful piece of land, which seemed like a very quiet place to be. But he was obsessed with noise. He said to me, "Can you believe it? I paid all this money for peace and quiet, and I am hearing noise from the road!" He wanted to sue the realtor who sold him this house because it was listed as peaceful. To him that meant that he was not supposed to hear any noise. The moment he moved in, he began listening for noise and put so much effort toward hearing it. Isn't that what we do all the time? We listen for noise. But do we ever listen to the silence in ourselves? Right now, if you listen, you can hear it. You will discover so much more if you hear that silence. The moment you hear that silence, the power of your internal voices weakens. But if you hate your thoughts and inner dialogue, they will never diminish. Therefore, the second door, the door of speech, is very important. As you hear the silence, you are able to host the chattering mind. As you host without judgment or analysis, the power of your inner voices dissipates.

FINDING INNER REFUGE THROUGH THE SPACIOUSNESS OF MIND

The third aspect of refuge is associated with the mind. The principles of body, speech, and mind are interrelated, but the mind is primary. Consider your sense of self. You have some idea of who you are. I'm not talking about the strong voice that says, "I am a professor," or "I am a mother." Let's look at the "three o'clock in the morning" voice. At that time the professor or the mother is sleeping and someone else is there. There is a sense of not knowing who you are rather than asserting that you are somebody. The asserting voice is the ego. It is more active, and so it is not hard to find. If you meet someone and have a ten-minute conversation, you have a good sense of who they think they are. That's not what is interesting here. More interesting is that they don't know who they are. There is a pervading dullness—the absence of knowing oneself—called ignorance. Do I know myself in this moment? Or is not-knowing present in me at this moment? You may say, "What do you mean by that? I can understand what you're saying, but . . ." That's a voice. But beyond that voice there is a sense of not knowing. It is not about not knowing the meaning of what I'm saying. I am talking about the root not-knowing—not knowing yourself. This pervades everything happening in your mind, in your speech, and in your activities. What don't you know? You don't know yourself. There is a traditional Bön prayer that is sung to one's teacher: "Bless me to recognize my true face with my own eyes." Some people might think this refers to their actual face, but this is not what the prayer refers to. It is not referring to appearance or to form. At the gym, people are interested in looking at their own form, face, and muscles. How many mirrors are there? How many mirrors do you have at home? What are you looking at? You are looking at your face, your hair, your body. Wouldn't it be nice if you could simply look in a mirror and recognize who you truly are?

We feel uncomfortable whenever we engage in doubt, when we lack confidence or lose our sense of direction. Those are the moments we face challenges. What can we do? I recommend taking the medicine I call spaciousness. How do we take the medicine of spaciousness? As before, draw your attention inside—not to the body, not to the voices, but to the mind itself. Instead of feeling stillness or silence, try to feel the spaciousness. Why is this important? The nature of mind is very spacious. The root texts in the Bön tradition describe the nature of mind as clear and luminous. All pain, confusion, and struggle that you feel are simply because you don't recognize the mind's true quality.

As you become still and silent, it is then easier to close your eyes and draw attention to your mind. You can feel space around and within that sense of not knowing. You can discover awareness in that ignorance. You recognize the light within that darkness. You don't try to renounce ignorance and find awareness. You are finding awareness within that ignorance. You are not living with the effort of trying to renounce that ignorance. Effort is becoming effortless. The mind that was not aware is now conscious of that state, that *base*. The moment you feel that, you feel incredible protection. You feel a sense of security, a sense of peace, a sense of balance. The notion of refuge is about really feeling protection. So the third door to discover inner refuge is the door of the mind, and that door is accessed through spaciousness.

Let's approach spaciousness from a place of contrast—for example, when we experience anger. When anger manifests, it can be very explosive. You can feel this in your body, your energy (also called wind, or *lung* in Tibetan), or your mind. In a moment of anger, spaciousness is not there. If you are angry with a person, you are focused on what that person did or said. Your attention is extroverted; you are probably not even connected to the person, but to what that person did. You feel vulnerable, and anger feels like your strength, your protection, and it becomes your attempt to get rid of the problem.

The most important thing at this moment is to enter refuge through the door of the mind. What do you do? Draw attention inward. Close your eyes; look inward. Feel the tension in your body and connect with your breath. Become focused on your breathing and emphasize breathing out. Do this for five or ten minutes. As you gradually feel more comfortable, look at the anger directly, not through the lens of thoughts and ideas. Nonconceptually draw open attention to that anger. Host the experience in spaciousness. When you look directly at the anger in this way, the anger cannot remain; it dissolves. But if you are looking at anger with just another form of anger—a disappointed mind or a judgmental mind—then anger won't disappear. It is important to observe the anger directly, to host the experience of anger in spaciousness without engaging in further thinking.

Many times when I instruct people to observe anger directly, they claim that the anger gets worse. That tells me that they are not observing directly or nakedly. They are not observing with open awareness. Instead, they are looking at anger with another form of anger, perhaps a subtler form. The commenting mind that is looking at the anger is more subtle, and seems smarter than that angry mind. It is convincing you that it is the solution. You may think that your judgment is awareness, but it is not. You are looking through judgmental eyes, not with the eyes of naked awareness. You ask,

"How do I know if I am looking through the right or wrong eyes? How do I know if I am making a right or wrong observation?" One way to know is to look at the result. If you are getting angrier or feeling more hopeless, you are looking with the wrong eyes. If you look with the right eyes—observing directly and nakedly—the anger will immediately lose its conviction and solidity. The medicine of stillness, silence, and spaciousness is so powerful that it doesn't take a long time to dissolve an obscuration, a disturbing emotion such as anger that obscures open awareness. If you look with the right eyes in any given moment, it does not take a long time to discover a clear and open mind. What takes time is for us to become familiar with seeing in this way, hosting our experience in the space of inner refuge and trusting this refuge.

If a light is brought into a dark room, the light is not concerned with how long the room has been dark. It will not comment, "This darkness has been here so long that it will take all weekend to clear it up." Neither is it true to say, "This darkness seems quite recent. My work will go more quickly." Light, or awareness, is instantaneous. It instantly dispels darkness or confusion. Desiring light doesn't help. Longing for light doesn't shorten its arrival, but it can be helpful if someone tells you that you are going in the right direction or points out that you are going in the wrong direction.

Let's explore how we observe, and what kind of awareness we are talking about when we refer to *open awareness*. For example, I can look at a flower and simply be there with my perception. I'm not saying anything about the flower, like that it is too red or not fresh enough. I am just experiencing the flower without judgment. As I continue to experience the flower in this way, the liveliness around this flower emerges. When the one who is looking is not engaging the thinking, moving, analyzing mind, he or she can perceive nakedly and directly and discover the perfection or completeness in the moment. This is the experience of *being* the refuge.

When you're connected to stillness, silence, and spaciousness, anything you perceive can be experienced directly and vividly because the judging or moving mind is not occupying the space.

A good example of the awareness I am referring to is an experience in ordinary life that is familiar to most parents. It is the example of a napping child. When you observe your young child sleeping, she is most beautiful. Your sleeping child is lying in such a casual, flexible position. And in the moment in which you gaze upon her, she is still. We love it when young children are still! Their gentle breathing is so quiet and sweet. We love the silence that surrounds this moment, because when they talk it is nonstop. It is so spacious in this moment that you can see your child radiating light. She is so cute that you almost want to wake her up!

The true challenge for any parent is when the child does wake up and is not still and silent, and certainly not that spacious. During these moments, can you go into that same space within yourself in which you saw the child in his or her perfection? In the midst of however noisy they are, can you go back into yourself and connect with the silence around which you experienced your napping child? Can you *be* that silence and experience your child from that place? Maybe your child is going crazy with movement and noise, but it is the same napping child you see. That is the beauty. You see in this crazy, noisy, moving child the perfection that was so obvious in the napping child because the stillness, silence, and spaciousness that were so evident before are still present within you. That is the realization, a small one that is a reflection of a big one. You could be quite sick or dying, and stillness is present. No matter what happens around you, it is not shaking you, because you have recognized stillness, silence, and spaciousness—and you *are* that.

As you continue to turn toward the refuge while you meet the challenges of your life, as you become more and more familiar with the spaciousness, awareness, and warmth of the refuge, you have an experience of *yourself* as the refuge—this is who you essentially are, and you gradually come to experience that everything is fine as it is. In the Bön tradition this is the essence of *dzogchen,* and these are the highest teachings. All is perfected in the moment. Nothing is missing. You glimpse it, taste it, and feel it. The moment you taste it, you recognize that you are fine. This supports you to feel fine in the face of changes, even those changes you fear most, such as loss of a loved one or your own death. You feel supported and unshakable in the refuge. What comes from outside is no longer a big deal. If there is something you need to let go of, you let go. If this is the moment you need to forgive somebody, you are fully able to do so, because you are completely generous. If this is the moment to die, you are ready. Where does this power come from? It comes from the inner refuge. In the boundless space of being, there is no fear and no fault. The space is full, complete, perfected.

Because we face challenges in our life, this motivates us to enter the refuge. Our challenges become the opportunity to connect with the source of being. Once you are in the healing space of refuge, even if difficult emotions and feelings arise, they will process automatically by themselves. They will come but will not shake you; they will dissolve by themselves, because you are holding that space. You *are* that space, that truth. That truth can never be affected by what is false. That truth can never be destroyed.

One of the most challenging things for us is to trust the inner space of being. We usually think of protection in terms of form. We attain security by accumulating money. We achieve power and protection from hostility by accumulating weapons. However, whatever we create and accumulate to feel safe doesn't really work, because it doesn't touch our underlying insecurity. We need to find some other solution. Eventually, everything we have created or that we possess, all that we think will secure our happiness, we have to let go of. When we face death, whatever we have accumulated in this life will be of no help. At that point the truest refuge is to discover the inner space of being.

In the Bön and Buddhist traditions we have examples of enlightenment in the form of the Buddhas, and we have living teachers to guide us on our path. We have scriptures and teachings to clarify our confusion, and we have our fellow practitioners, who help and inspire us. These four supports—the teacher, the Buddha, the texts, and the fellow practitioners—are referred to as outer refuge. Although they are important, their true significance is that they point to and represent inner knowing, the inner refuge.

Not many people stop for even a moment to discover stillness, few listen to the silence, and even fewer recognize the truth of emptiness or spaciousness. Yet how simple it is to recognize and benefit from the experience of the inner refuge. You don't need to read many books about emptiness or engage in philosophical discussions. You can just draw your attention inward. As you rest with your attention drawn inward, you may begin to hear many voices in your head. *I need silence,* you think. Okay, so don't talk back to the inner dialogue that seems to be running by itself. Begin to listen to the silence around and within those voices. Be aware of space. Perhaps you are having a very strong, active thought. *I am not feeling any space!* Stop. Don't think further. Feel the spaciousness around and within that very thought. The moment you connect with the space, the thought dissolves. The moment you hear the silence, the voice is gone. The moment you connect with stillness in your body, the tensions begin to release.

You can feel that things are coming up within you. As sensations, thoughts, emotions, or memories come into awareness, as you notice them arising within you, allow them all. Everything that comes eventually dissolves. Anything arising in open spaciousness dissolves in that spaciousness. That is why it is called inner refuge. Do you have to go anywhere? No. Do you have to take your laptop or cell phone or remember the address or number of the inner refuge? No. You have everything you need: your body, speech, and mind are the doors to the inner refuge, accessed through the experiences of stillness, silence, and spaciousness.

THE SOURCE OF ALL POSITIVE QUALITIES

How do positive qualities arise, such as love and joy, or positive actions such as caring for others, or being creative and productive? Being productive is important in life. It is hard to imagine being paid a nice salary for being still, silent, and spacious for eight hours a day. According to the teachings of Bön, the space of being is infinitely rich. It is the source of positive qualities, and the actions that express these qualities are beneficial. You will feel the infinite potential of the source within you as you begin to recognize and then trust openness. But your attention must be directed in the right way in order to recognize openness. You don't want to get lost in that open space; you want to be aware of that space. In the same way, you don't want to be lost in your pain; you want to be aware of your pain. Your awareness of openness reveals the greatest source of all antidotes and positive qualities. The teachings of *dzogchen* do not focus so much on *cultivating* positive qualities. The advice is to go directly to the source, openness itself, and discover that the qualities are already there. If you do that, then you don't have to work hard to feel love, for example; love is abundant in the open space of your being.

Happiness is not a product of working harder. We get exhausted and depleted from working so hard. When you connect with the space of refuge, you can feel you are recharging yourself. You are ready to give more, to receive more, to share more. That space of refuge is what we are referring to as a source of all the beneficial qualities that we need in life.

Turning Pain into the Path

It is most important to acknowledge the existence of our pain identity and to have the proper relation to it. Often, pain goes unrecognized. For instance, you could be sitting on a bench in a beautiful park waiting to meet a friend for lunch. Perhaps you are checking your e-mail on your phone without hearing the birds or seeing the play of light on the trees. Physically you are breathing, but you may have no connection with your body. You could be caught up in your thoughts about some work issues, strategizing various solutions. Nothing is truly fresh and alive when you are caught up in your habitual patterns of body, speech, and mind. And it is not that easy to recognize these habitual patterns unless your discomfort becomes more acute. There are many in-between moments in our lives when we are waiting for the next "event." These are excellent opportunities to turn to the refuge. We can be anywhere—in a business meeting or at a lovely celebration—and recognize that we are not fully present. The bottom line is that we are often distracted and disconnected from our own creative energies and from what the natural environment and others have to offer. Each of us can find many opportunities throughout the day to become aware of habitual disconnection and to shift our attention to the refuge.

Until you recognize your pain identity, whether you experience it as boredom, disconnection, or some other manifestation of discomfort, no path of healing is available. Recognizing pain is the first step on the journey to awakening the sacred body, authentic speech, and luminous mind.

Directly in the midst of a bored, confused, or agitated experience, simply draw your attention to your body, and experience the stillness that becomes available. As you find stillness again and again, you will begin to realize that it is always available. It is a matter of turning your attention to the right place. Finding stillness sounds so simple that perhaps you might think it is not very convincing as a remedy for your problems. And because it is so simple, it can take years or a lifetime for someone to make that shift of drawing attention inward to discover what becomes available when they do so. Many do not make that shift and will always perceive the world as dangerous and threatening. But if you are able to make that shift of attention again and again, it can cause a remarkable transformation of your experience of yourself and the world. It is important to know that at any given moment of challenge or pain, there is another way to experience that very moment. Connect with the fundamental stillness of being. It is already there, but unrecognized.

When there are competing internal voices, hear the silence. It is right there, within those voices. We do not listen to inner silence or have a good relationship to it. We are drawn again and again to the stimulation and distraction of inner dialogue, negotiating and rehearsing. And we are pleased when we come up with a good strategy. At other times we try not to think about something that is bothering us, and with effort, push it out of our minds, distracting ourselves with other things. Whether we arrive at what we consider a good strategy, or actively distract ourselves from thinking about something, it is all pain speech from the point of view of the inner refuge. As we listen to the silence that is truly available in any given moment, whether we are in the middle of a busy airport or sitting at a holiday dinner table, our inner voices dissolve. These are the moments when something fresh and alive becomes available.

When you struggle with so many thoughts and strategies, recognize the spacious, open aspect of the mind. Spaciousness is always available, since it is the natural state of things. But instead of relaxing into the natural mind, your attention tends to get drawn outward when you feel hurt, threatened, or angry about a particular person or situation. You end up feeling that if you don't do something immediately, things will go in a bad direction. The irony is that if you do not draw your attention to the spaciousness within you, and instead, continue to follow the strategies of reactivity, then you are only worsening your pain. When you are engaged in making a plan or worrying about whether something will work or not, this is all the activity of the pain mind. And the pain mind will never be the source of genuine relief from suffering.

I am not suggesting that you reject, control, or try to stop your thoughts. What you simply do is *allow them*. You look at thinking as it is. Instead of rejecting or pushing it away, you open to it; you go toward it with your focus, and as you get close to it, it is like trying to catch a rainbow. You go through it, and what you find there is just space. Or you feel space around and within that thought. You are neither rejecting the thoughts nor inviting the thoughts. The moment you feel spacious, the thought cannot sustain itself anymore. It is not there anymore. But if you reject it, that is another thought. And that thought is a kind of smart ego: *I am outsmarting that thought by observing it. Oh, there it is.* And there you are, talking to yourself, holding on to the credential of being the observer of thoughts.

The mind that strategizes is itself the creator of our suffering, and no matter how elegant or refined our strategy, it is still a version of the pain identity—and a more pernicious one at that, because it doesn't recognize itself as the creator of the problem. So instead of coming up with a winning strategy, we must shift our relationship with the pain mind entirely, and become aware of the spaciousness. Then we also allow the observer to dissolve as well. Now you may wonder, *What is left?* You must find the answer for yourself, by directly and nakedly observing. We need to look directly into our busy, thinking mind in order to discover the luminous mind. Fortunately, others who have gone before us have done it and have provided instructions and encouragement for us.

So first we need to acknowledge our pain and draw our attention to stillness, silence, and spaciousness. If our pain dissolves, much becomes available in the open space of being. But if our pain has not simply dissolved, we need a proper relationship with it. We need a caring relationship.

To use an example from ordinary life, let's say you are in trouble, need help, and turn to a family member for support. How do you feel supported? It is likely that you will feel supported by another if they make themselves available and simply listen to you. We feel less supported if they interrupt us to point out a few flaws in our logic and suggest ways we can improve. "You really got yourself into a mess here, and I feel I need to point a few things out to you. I can only help you if you will listen to me this time." Or perhaps somebody is anxious about what you are revealing to them. They may be more fearful of the circumstances than you are. Do you feel supported? No. You also feel no support when somebody is there physically but they are distracted or seem rushed for time. They look at their watch; they take a phone call—it is clear their mind is somewhere else.

We feel supported when somebody is fully present, open, nonjudgmental, available, caring, and silently attentive. And the silence that contains the fullness of presence is quite beautiful. Just having another sitting next to you or across from you in this way makes you feel supported.

The example I have just given, showing how one person can be supportive to another, illustrates exactly how you should treat yourself, in order to have a caring relationship with your pain. Be open as you experience your pain. Be nonjudgmental, silent, and fully present. Host your pain with warmth. If you do that, you will heal more quickly. Being present in this way may take some practice, for it is quite possible you will discover that you are constantly judging yourself. There is not a moment of silence to just be with the pain, allow the pain, feel the pain, and host the pain with openness. Instead, you try to control your pain, force your mind, judge your pain, and as a result you become even more nervous and agitated. Of course, this increases feelings of being isolated and unworthy.

Our ego separates us from direct experience. It is a reaction to a perceived threat. You think you are in relation with pain because you are experiencing pain, but actually the reactive ego has no real connection to the pain. That is the fundamental suffering of ego— it has no connection to what is. Pain can be experienced purely and directly. Simply allow the experience fully and feel it. Why would you do such a thing? Because awareness itself is true connection, and this true connection gives birth to the warmth of many positive qualities such as love, compassion, joy, and equanimity. Awareness is the key to the natural healing process.

As with self-healing, a most powerful communication occurs when you understand someone else's pain with open awareness. This is the experience of compassion. Compassion—the genuine wish to relieve others' suffering—is one of the greatest paths to enlightenment. If you truly listen to the pain of another, no matter who that person is, you will feel compassion. Discovering compassion often necessitates a shift in how we view someone, a shift from being constricted to being open, open to experiencing the pain of another. An ordinary example of shifting your perspective could go like this: Imagine you have been waiting for a friend to come over for a nice dinner that you have prepared. As it gets later and later, you become angrier and angrier. The person finally shows up shaking and says, "I had an accident on my way over and my car was totaled." What do you feel? In a second your accumulated anger dissolves. How is it possible? Because you have recognized someone else's pain. When you experience someone's pain, the platform of your logic dissolves. We all have the natural capacity to dissolve the structure that separates us from another. And when we understand someone's pain, the constricting defenses of ego melt. Likewise, when we experience our own pain without judgment, the constricting structure of ego melts. Awareness that is direct and naked is compared to the sun, and the warmth of awareness dissolves the solidified pain body the way the warmth of the sun melts a structure of ice. This warmth is the warmth of connection. In connection, positive healing qualities such as love and compassion are readily available.

Remedy for Pain: Three "Pills" of Inner Refuge

Let's explore how you could heal a painful experience by finding refuge through the three doors of body, speech, and mind. First, engage in a brief reflection and become aware of a challenge or issue in your life at this time. As you bring it to mind, notice how this issue lives in your body. Bring clear attention to any agitation or tension you may be experiencing. As you experience the sensations in your body, draw attention to being still. Focus on stillness. As you begin to feel stillness, the agitation begins to calm; as you continue to focus on stillness, the agitation releases. Continue to draw attention toward stillness and as you feel it, rest there. Stillness can become the doorway to experience a glimpse of the unbounded space of being, a deeper stillness that is always present. That deeper stillness is the medicine, for it gives access to a sense of unbounded spaciousness. Your agitation has become the path for liberation, and it is a matter of fully realizing that stillness is the access or doorway to integrate unbounded spaciousness into everyday life. I actually refer to this medicine of *stillness* as a "white pill," and I encourage my students to take the white pill frequently throughout the day.

Another aspect of pain can be experienced as the internal voices we generate. As you turn your attention inward and simply look at any discomfort you may be experiencing, what happens? Maybe you are thinking, *I am looking, but I'm not sure I really see it.* That is a voice. You are talking to yourself. Or you are saying, *It sounds very easy, but it is not that easy.* Again, you are talking. Or perhaps you are thinking, *Well, I can just look at my pain, but the other person never changes. I can look at my own experiences, but how does it help if the other person doesn't change?* Again, more talking. If you are talking to yourself in this way, you are not paying proper attention to your pain. Can you hear this as pain speech? Pain is the one talking and you are identifying with the pain. You are confused as to who you truly are. The moment you realize you are not the voice of your internal dialogue, you become free. How do you do that? You draw attention to the silence. Stillness and silence are two different doorways but lead to the same place—the inner refuge. Here, because of your internal dialogue, you listen to the silence. The moment you hear the silence, that voice of your pain has gone, and you can become aware of the unbounded space of being. That pain voice has become a path, and the silence is what you have realized. Now it is a question about maintaining that silence, nourishing that silence, fully realizing that silence, integrating silence with every voice and every sound. That is how you transform or turn that pain speech into the medicine of silence through which we recognize the unbounded spaciousness. I refer to the medicine of *silence* as the "red pill," and again, recommend that you take the red pill of silence frequently throughout the day.

At any given moment in which you look at your mind, it could probably be clearer than it is. Most of the time, we are not even aware of whether our mind is clear or not because we are focused on others or involved in inner stories or fantasies. When you bring your focus to your mind itself, even while feeling confused or disconnected, if you look at your mind in the right way, you can discover that the nature of mind is clear and luminous, and that it always has been. But if you are not looking directly at mind itself, if you are caught in the contents of your mind and identifying with the imagination of ego, you don't see the clear and luminous mind. If you look at the mind itself, it is clear. It can never be anything other than clear. There is no force in the universe that can obscure the nature of mind. There is no force in the universe that can destroy space. Space is always here; it is just a matter of drawing your attention inward and discovering the unbounded spaciousness of being. When the mind moves into thinking, as you become aware of that, bring your attention back to the spaciousness itself. It is always right here; you just haven't noticed or valued it. That is how you turn the confusion of your moving, thinking mind, into the path. I refer to discovering the medicine of *spaciousness* as taking the "blue pill." Whatever challenging thoughts and emotions you are experiencing, whether individually or collectively, the medicine of spaciousness is always available.

Everyone wants to get rid of fear. People who experience fear are even fearful of not getting rid of fear. But even while you experience fear, confidence is always there. In pure presence there is no fear or hope. Staying longer in open awareness is the way to develop confidence. Be in that space. When you feel agitated, bored, confused, or angry, take one of the three pills and reconnect with the inner refuge. Knowing that inner refuge is the antidote, you can begin to turn toward it and recognize it when it occurs. As you recognize this, you begin to trust your experience. You cultivate confidence by becoming familiar with the inner space of refuge. So if you start doing that just five minutes a day, and gradually increase to ten minutes, and then half an hour, you will have less fear. It is a direct method.

Even trusting that there is such a refuge helps. How do you know where to turn? When fear or anxiety dominates your mind, you don't know where to go. By turning toward stillness, silence, and spaciousness, you will feel some protection. Even if you cannot fully connect, trusting that space is there is a form of protection from fear. You will begin to taste the confidence that becomes increasingly available the more direct personal experience you have with the inner refuge. The reason the inner refuge overcomes fear is that the natural state is beyond fear. It is beyond fear because the unbound space of being is unchanging. So if you are aware of a deeper state in yourself that is unchanging, and become familiar with that deeper state, you naturally become less fearful.

The natural state of mind is beyond birth and death. At death, it is only ego that loses. We will explore this more fully later in the book, but for now we can say that being in that space is the experience of openness that is deathless, changeless. Nothing changes. So when I become more familiar with that particular aspect, when I taste this sense of changelessness, a deep confidence and peace become available. This is not a confidence produced by thinking or having a philosophical point of view. Rather, it is a direct experience that is possible by recognizing what is already here.

So with the pain body or identity, we "take the white pill" and turn toward stillness; with pain speech, we "take the red pill" and turn toward silence; and with the pain mind, we "take the blue pill" and turn toward spaciousness. As we enter the experiences of stillness, silence, and spaciousness, our pain becomes the path to liberation. Each condition transforms into a path that leads to our final liberation—connection with the changeless essence.

You may think this is an oversimplification or a watered-down instruction. Does it seem too simple to be true? The *dzogchen* masters explain that the true nature of mind is so close we cannot see it. We all know how much we love complicated things. Whatever is harder to get we think is better. For some people, the biggest problem is always wanting something they can't get, and because of that desire they cannot see what they already have. The simple but profound truth is that the greatest thing we have is this present moment. Therein lies the greatest richness possible. But we don't see or experience ourselves fully in the present moment.

So whenever you feel pain, just be with it. Be a good support to your pain. Have a warm presence that is completely open and, most important, nonjudgmental. Just be there hosting your pain. People in the West often have a problem with stillness, silence, and spaciousness. When you are still, then you start looking for a problem. When you are silent, others get suspicious and think there is a problem. When you are spacious, others may think you're not very bright. A cultural shock that I experienced when I first came to the United States was the mantra "I'm busy." Everybody says this. If you say, "I'm not busy," then something must be wrong with you. If someone asks, "What do you do?" and you reply, "Nothing much," that person will think, *Something has got to be wrong here. This is not normal.*

Perhaps in your first moments of turning toward stillness, silence, and spaciousness you might feel a little relief. Then you think, *I don't know if this is really going to help.* If you continue following that voice, definitely it will not help. It is very difficult to become free of that voice. You may reason, *Sure, I can do this. I can just sit with this. But what is this going to change in my life? How is this going to take care of a real problem like my broken car?* As you listen to the silence, you may become aware of some active voices within you. The truth is, the moment you begin listening to the silence, you will feel a connection to the space. But we simply have no good sense of how space nourishes us and how open awareness supports us. We have no clue about the nourishing power of awareness itself, and so we identify with the commentary that arises, indentifying with the "smart ego" that we feel is so necessary to manage and make sense of our experience.

Some of the most beautiful experiences I have with people are the moments when someone deeply connects to the silence. Within a very short time, tears come, forgiveness emerges, and strength, clarity, joy—amazing qualities—manifest. Where do these qualities come from? They freely and spontaneously emerge from recognizing the open space of being. This recognition gives birth to everything. Perhaps you are wondering why that didn't happen before. We don't recognize the space of being because the space was occupied; the space was obscured with your ego. If you have so many thoughts and so many voices, you have lost connection to the silence. If you experience so much agitation and movement, you have no connection to the stillness. How is something going to emerge from that space? The connection to space only comes when you acknowledge and care about the pain, which just means being open to it and hosting your experience. It is as simple as that.

When people clear their psychological mess or pain, they often say, "I have been working for all these years, and now I think this problem has finally cleared; it is gone." But clearing your pain or your confusion is only half of the journey. The second part of the journey, and probably the most important part of the journey, has not yet started.

Let's say you have had some obsessive thoughts for the last few days. Then suddenly you notice this pattern, you become aware of it, and without contributing or participating or judging, you simply open. Finally you just discover spaciousness in that thought that was occupying your mind. Now the thought is gone. Then you say, "Wow, this is beautiful! It's gone." Then what do you say? "Okay, what's next? What is the next thing I have to worry about?" The one who is worrying always finds a new topic. If you begin scanning your life to see if anything needs fixing, you will always find something. When you find something, you begin to worry again. If you catch that process of worrying and looking for a problem and can be directly aware of that thought process rather than the content, as you observe it directly, it clears by itself.

No matter what the pain, the medicine is stillness, silence, and spaciousness. You may protest, saying, "You have no idea about *my* pain. If I tell you my story, then you will think differently." No, I won't. When I was growing up in India I saw a lot of Indian movies. And all of these Indian movies had the same story. Five minutes into the movie you would know how the movie was going to end. Our pain is like that. In the end, the core of everyone's suffering is very simple, but whether or not our pain liberates us depends on whether we acknowledge that simplicity.

Acknowledging and caring for pain is very important. When I use these words *acknowledge* and *care*, you might think we are dealing in mere concepts. But transforming pain into the path of liberation from pain is not a conceptual path. It involves nonconceptual awareness. It is just being open, hosting your experience in boundless space with arms of light.

I don't think there is anything like the awareness of space to process emotion. That space is such an incredible processor. There is no analysis equal to the processing capacity of open awareness. When you are trying to analyze something, you don't realize that the analyzer itself is part of the problem. Both the problem and the analyzer are constructions of the mind. But direct, open, naked awareness is not a construction of the mind but the nature of mind itself, and therefore is the greatest processor ever. If you *are* that awareness, everything is fully experienced. There is no unfinished business.

The beautiful thing about the open space of being is that it doesn't change because somebody calls it this name or that name. And when you experience that open space of being, it is important not to call it anything. Calling it something will interfere with connecting. A name should serve only to lead the mind there, but the name is clearly not the experience or the knowing itself, and in that sense the name is a block. It can serve to get close, but in the end, the name itself is an obstacle. Awareness has no name, no author or owner.

Another beautiful thing about spacious awareness is that it is like light. And as light, it does not recognize the history of darkness—how long, how intense, or how complex the darkness is. Light simply illuminates darkness. Light is not saying, "Okay, let's see about your particular darkness. Just how long have you been in the dark? And how many people have been in as dark a place as you have?" No matter how much confusion you experience, light does not recognize that. That is what is beautiful about awareness. Like the sun, it is not selective; the moment it shines, darkness is dispelled. The moment you are aware, the confusion of ignorance is dispelled.

Sometimes people have great experiences in meditation. Then they say, "Well, of course, this is only a momentary experience and it's not as real as my pain. After all, my pain has a long history. This relief cannot be real. At the moment I am feeling great, but surely this can't be real." Isn't it amazing that you can feel so spacious one moment and the next moment completely doubt the experience? The moment you begin to feel your pain, you proclaim, "Ah yes, now this is a familiar place. I knew that bliss couldn't have been real." As the old saying goes: A familiar hell is better than an unfamiliar heaven. That is a common experience for many people. When they feel pain, they say, "Yes, now I'm back home. This is it. This is me. This is my karmic cushion. It smells right. It feels familiar. I guess this is my lot in life."

Sit and draw full attention to your body and connect with the physical experience of stillness. Don't hold your breath, just breathe. Listen to the silence, especially when you are talking internally. That internal voice is an opportunity to find silence. So be open to that voice, allow that voice, and feel the silence in it. The moment you hear inner silence, the voice of your pain speech loses power. And resting in the silence is a very distinctive experience. If you look at your conceptual mind, the thought you are having at this very moment, even a thought such as *Oh, I'm listening to the silence,* can obscure spaciousness. If you identify with the thinking mind, it actually blocks potentiality and creativity. So rather than rejecting your thoughts or being excited by them, just simply be open and feel the spaciousness around and within them. Find and continue to recognize spaciousness. In spaciousness, host your experience. When awareness comes alive, thought dissolves. Your ideas no longer dominate your experience. You are more flexible. You are more spacious. You have more chance to grow. You have more chance to become creative. You have a chance to evolve.

In the end, through stillness, silence, and spaciousness we arrive at the same place, the natural mind. But on the path they are different because you arrive through a particular door: one through movement, one through voice, one through thought. Although the paths are different, in essence they are the same. When you arrive, there is no distinction between whether you came through one door or another. It is no longer important where you came from. The door is only important when you are lost. If you are lost on the eastern side of the mountain, then it is better that you find the eastern path, because it is the closest to you. Of course, you can always wander around to the west, but the recommendation would be to find the closest door. When we fly we are always reminded by the flight attendant that "the nearest exit could be right behind you." In this case, the closest entrance is right within you. Your inner critic could be the closest entrance and remind you to enter the inner refuge through hearing the silence. The tension in your jaw could be your closest entrance and remind you to enter the inner refuge through stillness. Your doubting, hesitating mind could be the closest entrance to recognizing the spaciousness of mind. But we do love to complicate things and will often choose the furthest possible route. It is curious, how we don't value that which is closest.

THREE PILLS A DAY: REINFORCING THE HABIT OF TURNING INWARD

Why is it so difficult to bring clear and open attention inward, even if we agree it is a good idea? Because we are not very familiar with openness and we don't trust it enough. We doubt it will work or we doubt that we are sufficient in the core of our being. Therefore, we don't turn to our essence and don't fully experience the richness of our being. Even if we do have an experience, our smart ego interferes and diminishes the experience, saying, "It can't be that easy."

How can we become more familiar with inner refuge? If we are given a prescription for medicine that is absolutely necessary for our health, we are motivated and will find a way to remember to take it. So perhaps we need to think of turning toward inner refuge as a necessary medicine. This is why I use the analogy of the three pills: the pill of stillness, the pill of silence, and the pill of spaciousness. Treat this as a prescription that you really need—not only to treat your sickness, but also to support you to flourish as a human being.

If you pay attention, the opportunity to take one of the pills chooses you. When you are restless and agitated, your agitation has chosen you. At that very moment you can be grateful for your agitation, for it has reminded you to take the white pill of stillness. Just breathe in slowly and go toward your agitation with full openness and feel it. Your stillness is right in the midst of your agitation. Don't distract yourself and reject the agitation, trying to find stillness somewhere else. Simply go toward it. Discover the stillness right there within your agitation.

The moment you hear complaint in your voice, you can recognize it as the time to take the red pill of silence. What do you do? Be open. Host your complaints as you hear the silence within your voice. Silence is within your voice because silence is the nature of sound. Space is the nature of matter. Don't look for stillness by rejecting movement. Don't search for silence by rejecting sound. That is not possible. You can never find it by rejecting your experience.

When your mind is going crazy with thoughts and plans, take the blue pill of spaciousness. Remember, don't look for space by rejecting your thoughts; space is already there. But it is important to make that discovery, again and again.

So make sure you take the three pills throughout the day. Take these pills as often as you recognize the opportunity, but my recommendation is to consciously choose, at least five times a day, to connect with the inner refuge by taking one of the pills. That is my prescription for you. It seems useful and necessary to prescribe a specific number of times to encourage familiarity with this informal meditation practice. By remembering to take the three pills, you will begin to discover the powerful benefits of the inner refuge.

CHAPTER TWO

INNER REFUGE AND DISCOVERING THE SACRED SELF

I wrote three verses as a teaching on the inner refuge to encourage my students to honor and respect our ordinary body, speech, and mind as the doorways to discovering our inherent positive qualities. The first verse corresponds to the refuge of the body, the second to the refuge of the dimension of speech, and the third to the refuge of the mind. When pain body, pain speech, and the pain mind are acknowledged and hosted in the stillness, silence, and spaciousness, they naturally dissolve and release. Through this, we discover the enlightened or sacred dimensions of body, speech, and mind. I refer to these sacred dimensions as the body of emptiness, the body of light, and the body of great bliss.

(You may listen to me reciting these verses in Tibetan and in English on Tracks 1 and 2 of the CD.)

Inner Refuge

Body
The center of the victorious mandala, one's own body,
The source of all positive qualities without exception,
Is the expanse within the three channels and the five chakras.
I take refuge in this body of emptiness.

Speech
All the gathered clouds of suffering and misery
Are completely cleared by the wisdom wind,
Revealing the unelaborated, primordially pure expanse of the sky.
I take refuge in this body of light.

Mind
From the pavilion of the five wisdom lights,
Rays from nondual spheres of light emanate,
Clearing the webs of the darkness of ignorance.
I take refuge in this body of great bliss.

FIRST REFUGE: THE BODY OF EMPTINESS

The body of emptiness can be accessed through our experience of the physical body. In general we can focus upon the body as a whole and discover the experience of stillness. As we are still, the stillness is the doorway through which we can experience the unbounded, unchanging space of being. We can also focus on the space within our heart or upon a more elaborate "sacred architecture" of the body using three channels (internal channels for the flow of subtle energy) and five chakras (energy centers), and discover the unbounded space there. By focusing clearly and finding stillness, we can discover an experience of unbounded spaciousness.

Space can be experienced in this body, in these chakras, in these channels, and particularly in our heart. So we draw our attention to our own body, our physical body. "The mandala of one's own body" is not a metaphor, but refers to this very body that we have—this physical body. Every aspect of our physical body is sacred. What determines whether we experience the "ordinary" body or the "sacred" body depends upon the perceiver. If the perceiver is the thinking, moving mind, we will experience ordinary pain and pleasure. If we engage the experience of *being*, nakedly and directly, we will discover the sacred body, the body of emptiness. Whether we use awareness of our whole body, or five chakras, three channels, or our heart to host the awareness of this sacredness, there, in that internal space, the body of emptiness abides. That is who I am, a being of stillness. I am the body of emptiness. When I experience that body of emptiness, I take refuge in my true being. I am the refuge.

The body of emptiness has incredible qualities: indestructible, changeless, deathless, unconditioned, and pervasive. These are the qualities that your ordinary body provides the opportunity to experience. Who you truly are is indestructible and changeless. Our essence is changeless. And through stillness, the body of emptiness is discovered in this physical body, particularly in your physical heart. In these teachings, the physical heart is very sacred. Our true being and energy abide in the sacred space within the heart. So that is where we go for refuge. That is where we focus our searching mind and allow our doubts and questions to exhaust themselves. Just simply draw your attention within, become still, and feel the deep stillness that is always there. You can never lose it, because you *are* it. The ability to go inward needs to be practiced. Again and again we draw our attention inward and trust that place of stillness with an attitude of respect. This is our practice.

Throughout the history of humankind, people have been revering and bowing before sacred mountains, images of gods and goddesses, and shrines. We have made offerings with great respect and awe and have prayed for guidance. That is the attitude you want to have for the space within at this very moment. Whether the entrance to this moment of experience is chaotic and noisy or serene and sublime makes no difference. What is important is your attitude of respect and your ability to draw unwavering attention inward and become conscious of stillness. Having trust and respect is a conventional sense of refuge. Bowing, making offerings, and feeling joy and inspiration toward the refuge of your being is another conventional sense of refuge. *Being* that stillness, *being* that space, is the ultimate sense of refuge. Both the conventional and ultimate aspects of refuge are important to have in order to awaken the luminous mind.

Start with humbleness toward yourself. People are very self-critical, comparing themselves with others and competing with them. What if you spoke to another person aloud the way you talk silently to yourself? Isn't it likely that you would be seen as abusive? Too many of us treat ourselves harshly and lack self-respect. It is important not to be aggressive or critical toward oneself or to diminish one's worth. Self-respect is both the prerequisite for and the result of refuge: the attitude necessary for taking refuge, and the conventional benefit of taking refuge. The ultimate benefit is that when you take refuge, you feel a sense of being at home in yourself. You also feel protected. It is a deep protection in the space of being—the changeless, indestructible space, which is who you truly are. That is the key message here: when you turn toward this inner refuge and when you *are* that, you experience the power of changelessness.

If you examine why you feel painful emotions and why you are anxious, it has so much to do with fearing change. Whether we are experiencing small changes in life related to relationships, work, or family, or bigger changes such as serious illness, aging, or dying, change makes us aware that the expectations of ego are unfulfilled. Our ego, our conventional sense of self, has difficulty adapting to change. Fear of new situations thus has to do with our relationship to change. From a deep place we fear that "I" will change. That sense of "I" is the fundamental error. It's not really because somebody left me or I lost my job that I feel pain. The real pain is the fear that whatever is happening is changing *me*—I am losing something I thought was permanently mine. My "I" has been attacked. The "I" who is fearful is the changeable "I," the false ego.

The only medicine for this changeable pain identity or ego is to glimpse the changeless essence. How can the changeless essence be altered? If changelessness is my true essence, no one has the power to destroy it. Again, this cannot just be a belief but must be a direct experience. The benefit of this recognition is not theoretical. Even a glimpse of this is powerful. You open your heart as you turn toward the inner refuge with a sense of trusting openness, and that brings you closer to experiencing a glimpse of changelessness. The moment you glimpse changelessness, you experience everything as it is. You are at peace with what is. That is how the space of refuge protects. Protection is not a fantasy in which mythical beings show up with magical weapons and fend off everything that is making problems for you. Rather it is the inner strength that has no face or form or weapon. It is nothing and therefore it is everything. It is formless and the most powerful strength you can discover. Turning to stillness and discovering the inner space within your body is the way you become the first refuge, the body of emptiness.

Second Refuge: The Body of Light

The second refuge states: "I take refuge in the body of light." The body of light refers to clarity or luminosity, consciousness, awareness—awareness of that indestructible space, awareness of the first refuge. Awareness is supremely important. It gives birth to whatever quality is needed in any given situation and provides much more than the ego could ever imagine. The awareness of space *is* knowing. This awareness is not awareness of an object, but awareness itself, awareness without author or owner. It is the vividness and liveliness of each moment, nakedly perceived.

"All the gathered clouds of suffering and misery" in the second verse of my refuge poem is a metaphor for the result of failing to recognize the clear and open space of being. The open, clear, and spacious sky is a metaphor for your being; the light that pervades the sky is a metaphor for awareness of being. In the natural world, clouds obscure the sunlight, and when the sunlight is obscured, whatever needs light and warmth will not flourish. Similarly, without the awareness of the space of being, we do not receive the nourishment we need in order to flourish as human beings.

There is a subtle wind that is connected with the awareness of the space of being. That is called the wisdom wind. This subtle wind supports the experience of the release or dissolution of pain and the glimpse of openness. In that glimpse of openness—that subtle movement within our consciousness—the clouds of suffering part. The awareness of openness is not obscured. This wind is not only a metaphor, but can be directly experienced. (For more detailed explanations of the channels and chakras and of the winds, see my book *Awakening the Sacred Body*, which includes meditation practices that clear the negative, obscuring winds and allow the wisdom wind to move.)

When the clouds of obscuration clear, there is light. This is the light of awareness. Internally, you are able to experience pure awareness. So we take refuge in awareness itself. Awareness is the direct cause for many qualities. Openness allows all our experiences, but awareness gives brightness to appearance. The sky allows, but the sun has more of a role in what you see right now. In terms of our inner experience, qualities such as compassion, joy, and love are linked with the presence of awareness as the immediate cause. The root cause of positive qualities is openness or space, but only when awareness of that space is present does the quality emerge. So many feelings become available because of being conscious, being aware of the space of being. It is possible to be open before being aware of it, but the moment you become aware of openness, it gives birth to positive qualities. I am making a distinction between openness and being aware of openness. Openness can exist whether you are aware of it or not, but when you are aware of openness, it gives birth. That is the reason we take refuge in the light, in awareness.

Let me try to express this in another way. If you are in the country and walk outside at three or four in the morning, it is dark. You can't distinguish the objects or colors of the natural environment around you. While you may not perceive the details of the trees, birds, and flowers, nonetheless those things are there. The space is still holding everything, but you are not able to see anything. You may be able to imagine there are many beautiful things in this space, but you are not seeing them. You can imagine what surrounds you, and trust what is there because you remember what you experienced previously. Then, when morning comes, the sun rises and reflects on your surroundings, and you see the beauty of trees, mountains, grasses, flowers. Perceiving the beauty gives you access to the inner qualities. In *dzogchen* teachings we hear so many times that everything is perfected in the base of one's being, the inner space of being. We may read or hear this many times, but until the sun shines, until you are aware of that inner space of being, you don't see the perfection.

When the light of awareness shines, you are able to experience what is perfected. Genuineness and authenticity come from this union of openness and awareness. You see what is here. You take refuge in this body of light. You turn your focus inward and take refuge in awareness itself.

This body of stillness, emptiness, and this body of awareness, light, has nothing to do with any religion or philosophy, but it has everything to do with you. It is within you. Look directly within and you will see it. Look away and it is obscured. Why do we look away? Ego is not able to see it. Ego only sees its own imagination. Who sees it then? It sees itself. It knows itself. Therefore it is called self-realization. I already referred to one of the lines of supplication in the Bön and Buddhist traditions that express this as a sincere intention and request from the student to the teacher. I've included a few more: "Bless me to recognize my true face with my own eyes. Help me to recognize the treasure within, the refuge tree, the jewel, the source of enlightenment, my true self." There is no knowledge greater than that recognition, and we cannot produce it or make it happen through any effort. That recognition is the greatest gift you can have in your life, and we acknowledge that in prayer.

THE THIRD REFUGE: THE BODY OF BLISS

The third place of refuge is in the body of great bliss. When awareness arises, something happens. From the space in your heart, from the light of awareness, the darkness of ignorance is dispelled, and a sense of great bliss manifests. Great bliss is simply the joy of being. It is not the joy of accomplishing or the joy of having or the excitement or expectation of having. You are, and at this point you know you are, therefore you are joyful. You are joy. You don't have to feel joy because you are joy. You don't have to look for joy because you are joy. You don't even try to give joy because you are giving already. You don't have to share because you are already giving by being. The more you *try* to give, the less you are able to give. The more you *are,* the more you give. You are fully present. You are that bliss; you are that joy; you have that recognition and you don't have to try to do anything. That sense of joy is where we go for refuge. It is possible that we might not have connected with such joy, or we might only have glimpsed the experience, but nevertheless it exists in us. Therefore, we take refuge in the presence of joy in us.

The result of taking refuge is certainty and confidence, inner peace, and the abundance of positive qualities. Deep confidence means that you are that stillness, you are that silence, you are that spaciousness. Genuine confidence does not come from our thoughts. It is not an internal cheering section saying, "Yes, you are good enough, you are loved, you are great, you are going to win." Confidence comes from the realization that there is nothing to lose. That is true strength, strength that does not come from hope as opposed to fear. Hope and fear are the food of ego. When you experience deep confidence, you are free of hope and fear. No matter what you encounter in life, you don't lose what you are. If you are still, you become that fully; if you hear silence, you become that completely; if you recognize spaciousness, you are that insepa- rably. In this way we overcome the root of the suffering of our pain body; we overcome the three poisons of aversion, attachment, and ignorance; and we achieve the three bodies of emptiness, light, and bliss. The realization of these three bodies is the fruit of meditation, and the fruit is already in us.

Since the fruit or result is already in us, it is important to emphasize that you don't make the result, but you discover the presence of the result. If you have to make a positive result, forget about it. It is impossible. No intelligence can make that result through any effort imagined or unimagined. It is already there, so it is a question of discovering it. This is the *dzogchen* view. And meditation is the path or means of recognizing that view. The conditions and challenges in everyday life are our opportunities to discover again and again the truth of the view—that each moment is complete as it is. Through becoming familiar with your natural mind, you gain complete confidence in the presence of the three enlightened bodies—the body of emptiness, body of light, and body of great bliss—in yourself.

In contrast to recognizing these three bodies of refuge in ourselves, our ordinary mind is most familiar with the pain body, pain speech, and the pain mind. Often we not only experience pain, we feel we *are* pain. We identify with pain, and we are not even aware we are identifying with pain. We may try to love our spouse or children, but are not really able to truly love or share joy because we don't feel it. And we don't feel it because we don't have access to the open space of being. We identify with pain or discomfort, and that is all that we experience. Still, we try to give what we don't have. We try to give joy and end up giving sadness. We try to give love and end up giving anger or frustration. We try to open, and realize we are closing. This is stressful and effortful, and often people feel guilty because they think they should be more loving. Why is it so difficult? Because you can only give what you are connecting with in the moment. At such a time it is important to realize that rather than trying to produce a quality you don't experience, you first need to *clear* the obscured space in which you experience yourself, the space that is obscured by frustration and thoughts and feelings and stories. At these moments, efforts to express love are wasted. Sadly, people can spend years and years of their lives with fruitless effort and end up feeling disconnected from themselves and inauthentic in their expressions.

If you really want to connect with and realize the benefits of openness, it is necessary to recognize the pain identity, the one who puts so much effort into being something other than who you are. Sometimes we feel that if we didn't make an effort, we would just be a selfish, irritable, or sad person. But often we fail to realize that our effort to push or change ourselves is still an expression of the suffering we experience, and if we bring our attention directly to a moment of effort, something else becomes available—a big shift can take place. When you look directly inward, and nakedly connect with the openness that is always available, a new face will be seen, new qualities will emerge. If the qualities don't emerge right away, you need to host your pain with arms of light as long as necessary. Only when the pain dissolves and the openness is recognized can you share the positive qualities so abundantly present there. When you discover a connection to a deeper authentic space within, the quality you are seeking will be found. You will find something you could never have produced through any effort imaginable. Effortless positive qualities spontaneously arise when you are open and aware.

The foundation of refuge is trust. Even if you don't have access to a deep experience of stillness and the body of emptiness in a given moment, you can still trust that it is there. There may be times in your life when you are going through much pain, fear, confusion, and darkness, and you feel there is no light. Rather than saying, "I don't see or feel it; it is not there," you could say, "I don't see any light, but I trust that it is there. I don't feel it in this moment, but I trust that it is there." That trust offers protection, even though you have no realization of inner peace at the moment. That trust gives you some strength and direction to contain those difficult experiences better.

Your challenges will not overwhelm you completely, thanks to the power of your trust. There may be moments when you don't feel still. There is so much agitation and confusion, and so many thoughts and emotions and voices in your head. For you, there is no openness; there is no awareness; there is no bliss. You feel occupied with distractions of all kinds. But still you can trust. "I don't have the strength to feel stillness or awareness or feel any bliss, but I trust it is here." Trust that essence. Trust yourself. At those times the refuge poem can comfort you by encouraging and reminding you that there is a place within you that is trustworthy.

CHAPTER THREE

THE GIFTS OF INNER REFUGE

How do we personally benefit from the gift of refuge, and how can it benefit others? The body of emptiness, body of light, and body of great bliss are aspects of our being. We all have these three bodies in ourselves, but our realization of this is obscured. Through the practice of meditation with the three doors—recognizing and resting in stillness of the body, silence of speech, and spaciousness of mind—we release our pain identity and have clear access to space, awareness, and warmth.

When we connect with this clear space of being, it is not a passive process. As we meditate, we are not simply becoming a disinterested observer of our thoughts and feelings as they float by. Rather, we are recognizing the space of our very being itself, and this intimate recognition is a spark, a light that ignites a positive response to the moment. As we draw clear and open attention inward, we are healed and nourished in so doing, and we naturally become generous. When you abide in openness, awareness, and warmth, you are naturally able to express generosity, experience forgiveness, feel love, or have compassion. The single experience of resting in the refuge gives birth to so many positive experiences. According to the *dzogchen* teachings, if you abide in the inner refuge, positive action will naturally arise. It is not that you need or want to give; rather, generosity spontaneously arises because nothing is obscuring or blocking it from arising.

Let's look at each of the three refuges referred to in the poem in Chapter 2—body of emptiness, body of light, and body of great bliss—and the distinct gift that each has to offer.

THE GIFT OF OPENNESS: THE BODY OF EMPTINESS

As you practice drawing your attention again and again to stillness, it is important to allow your thoughts and feelings to arise without judging or changing them in any way. As you simply host whatever you experience in openness, and continue to maintain awareness of the openness itself, this sense of unbounded self that you experience not only is a gift that benefits you, but can also be a great gift to another. You have the power to let others be as they are. As you feel that unbounded space in yourself, you allow others to be, without having to manage or manipulate yourself or them. You are able to allow their experience fully because you can allow your own experience fully. Whenever family, friends, or co-workers express stress, tension, fears, or expectations, you are able to be there fully without judging or reacting. If you do not feel that space in yourself, how can you give it to anyone else? But if you do experience the unbounded space of the first inner refuge, it becomes a great gift to offer to another. Their experience, whether joy or suffering, does not activate your pain body, and so you are able to offer them openness. The openness that gives rise to confidence and fearlessness within you can inspire others to discover their own sense of confidence.

Perhaps you have been trying to help a particular person in your life, but your efforts are unsuccessful or have led to tension or misunderstanding. If you look closely at the situation, you will see that your pain body is being activated in response to that person, and this causes your words or actions to come off as controlling and manipulative instead of caring and supportive. Sometimes even our good intentions conceal a wish to control others. Any sense of discomfort within you is a clear sign that you need to go back within and connect with the refuge of unbounded space. You need to feel that space within yourself first, before you can influence others positively. As you experience inner space, you will naturally radiate a sense of spaciousness by your very presence. As you become aware of that unbounded space, as you feel and connect with that unbounded space, you impart the gift of openness by allowing others to be who they are. It is not that you give someone space by going away and leaving them alone; rather, you are fully present with them, while allowing them space to be as they are. The space of refuge is not given by anyone to anyone else; it is a naturally existing gift. To recognize this gift is to receive it. It is simply the *recognition* of this gift that has been lacking. I am reinforcing the idea that inner refuge is a gift that you both receive as well as offer to others. When you are in the refuge, the gift is naturally there. As you recognize this gift, not only is everything you need right there within it, but as you connect with this sense of richness and worthiness within yourself, you will naturally become aware of opportunities to benefit others. All positive qualities arise spontaneously from this inner space and become available in our interactions with others. But it is important to know that we are not *trying* to give. This is not a dualistic process in which one person is the active, enthusiastic giver while the other is a passive, needy receiver. No, the entire process is beautifully empty. Knowing this, you become infinitely generous. This is the gift of openness—the body of emptiness referred to in the poem of inner refuge.

Overcoming Fear with the First Refuge

As we discussed in Chapter 2, our human ego is changeable and vulnerable. Even though we all have the capacity to recognize the changeless essence, we grasp at our temporary experience with our conceptual mind in an attempt to protect ourselves from loss or change. We want what is by nature changeable to be unchanging. This creates an identity of insecurity, which I have been calling the pain body. We seek refuge in the wrong place, the changeable pain body. Our desire is that it should be changeless, and when this expectation is repeatedly disappointed, we experience fear. The continuous habit of identifying ourselves with what is changeable is the source of fear.

The first refuge, the body of emptiness, is the changeless essence, the unbounded space of being. In reality, you are changeless, and you come to recognize this when you experience the first refuge. Recognizing it does not mean, "I intellectually believe this to be true." Rather, you experience it so directly that the reality of it is without doubt. This recognition of the unbounded, unchanging space of being is a powerful experience of openness, and becomes the source of your inner confidence. Because you directly experience the changeless essence, this protects you from the fear of change—even the most extreme change that ego faces: death.

Every time we go to the first refuge through the door of stillness, we can have a taste of changelessness. This taste is the medicine that heals fear and anxiety. To explore this, engage in a short period of reflection, bringing to mind a recent experience of anxiety or insecurity. Form a clear intention to seek refuge through the door of stillness. As you host the experience of fear or anxiety, bring unwavering attention to the stillness, until you glimpse unbounded spaciousness. Trust this glimpse. As you trust, your fear or anxiety begins to dissipate. Rest your focus in the openness that you discover. Rest there as long as the experience is fresh. In the beginning, you may be able to experience maintaining an open focus for only a short period of time—perhaps a few minutes. As you continue to practice hosting any fear or anxiety while focusing on stillness, you will again and again witness the dissolution of the anxiety and be able to rest in openness for longer periods. As you practice this, your fear can be overcome by trusting, and then resting in openness, which *is* the changeless, unbounded space of being—the body of emptiness. Confidence will naturally become available as you continue to practice resting in openness. This is the real and only way to go beyond fear and discover natural confidence.

THE GIFT OF AWARENESS: THE BODY OF LIGHT

As we discussed in Chapter 2, the second refuge—refuge in the body of light—is awareness of the unbounded space of being. When we discover the inner refuge of awareness, we connect with a sense of completeness, fullness, and worthiness. This is a tremendous gift and an antidote for so much of the suffering that we experience, whether it takes an extreme form like physical addictions or a more subtle form, such as depending on external things for our happiness, a strategy that is doomed to eventual failure. When you experience awareness of inner spaciousness, you feel complete in the moment, vividly present, and connected as you are and where you are. It is the experience of self-worth in the truest sense. You realize you are full with potential. Because every individual in any given moment has infinite possibilities within him or her, when you extend the gift of awareness to others, you allow them to feel, explore, and discover who they are, without trying to control or manipulate their process or result.

Suppose you are in a relationship with another person who is experiencing some challenge or confusion. You may feel their discomfort. If it activates your pain body, your reaction will not be coming from a connection with infinite possibility, and so will lack creativity. Your ego is not able to fully help, because it lacks space, awareness, and warmth. Whenever you recognize that ego has been triggered, it is important to connect with the inner refuge. Otherwise, even with good intentions, ego interferes with your own or somebody else's process. If you truly want to help another, keep ego's agenda out of it. Let others feel and connect and figure out their process. That does not mean that you remain passive and disengaged; on the contrary, you are fully present.

My son Senghe is five as I write this. He often asks for my attention, regardless of whether I am busy or not. One time he asked me to come into the living room where he was playing. I entered the room with my sandals on and he immediately said, "Take your sandals off!" By saying this, he was asking me to sit down and be with him. To him, my wearing sandals meant that I was ready to go at any moment. Of course, once I took off my sandals and was sitting with him, he was not paying any attention to me! Still, he wanted my presence there. He was fully engaged in playing and not asking me to do anything, but my presence meant something to him. The gift of the second refuge is just this: be present with full attention without interfering with whatever is happening. I find it interesting to observe the responses of children to the adults around them. Young children naturally respond to the openness and playfulness of adults, and react when adults are distracted or judgmental or have their own agenda.

Sometimes we are not good listeners to others around us. Why? We have too much internal dialogue. We are distracted or more interested in listening to the voices of our own ego than bringing clear attention to someone else. Just allow another to express, to feel, and to explore. Be fully present with them. Do not underestimate the power of connecting in this way. With the second refuge you are not sitting in a passive, quiet place but are engaging with awareness, whatever arises. Being present without a judgment or an expectation of someone is a great gift. Of course, if you cannot experience this in yourself, if you have not truly received this gift of awareness, it is difficult to give this to another.

Overcoming Hope with the Second Refuge

The second refuge overcomes hope. This idea may seem surprising, since hope is considered a virtue in Western religion—an expectation of future blessings and an antidote to despair. But sometimes, without our realizing it, our hopes disguise a hidden fear of lack within us. If we look at how hope can work in this negative way in our lives, we have to ask ourselves what we are hoping to receive from others. How often do we find ourselves wanting those around us to change, and how often are we able to justify reasons why they should? If you are honest, you will discover the reason you hope someone else will change is that you experience some lack or some dissatisfaction within yourself. Often we hope someone else will fulfill a neglected aspect or compensate for a perceived lack in ourselves. When we do not have a connection to the inherent completeness of our own lives we often look to others to provide it for us. So it is important to connect with awareness to the space of being, and to discover richness in ourselves, the sense of the infinite possibility of each moment. When we do, we find that not only do we need less from others, but we have much more to offer them.

Hope can be a good thing. "It is my hope that you should be happy!" We hold the possibility of someone's wellness and happiness in our good wishes. But the shadow of this can be, "I don't get why you are sad for this long." Sometimes hoping for someone's happiness comes from not accepting that the person is going through what they are going through. If you allow them to acknowledge and feel their pain, they will heal much faster than if you interfere and do not allow them to feel.

Perhaps you had an argument or a falling out with someone. You were trying to say or do something for them, and they misinterpreted your intention or didn't like it and got angry with you. Now you expect the other person to apologize, and you are waiting for that person to make the first move. In families, these frozen stances can even last for years. If you find yourself in such a situation, it is important to realize that you are allowing weakness and confusion to influence you, instead of coming from your strength. If you turn to the inner refuge and connect with your inherent strength, you can overcome this shared pain body and take the healing initiative.

Entering the fullness of being through direct, naked awareness is a much better path to bliss than waiting around for someone else's apology or attention. Just go to the refuge directly. Make it part of your everyday life, and you will find that you live with very little regret or unfinished business. If you look closely at what you are asking from somebody else, you will discover you already have it. You already have richness, you already are full; you have that connection, so in some sense it doesn't make any sense to ask another for it. Would you ask for something you already have? Furthermore, once you discover your inherent richness, you might feel compassion for the other person. You might recognize that they are not connected to their own richness. The only way compassion will come is by shifting something in yourself and realizing that you *are* what you seek from another. You are the second gift, the gift of awareness.

If you want to explore how this gift of awareness, the gift of the second refuge, can work in your life, reflect and bring to mind a relationship where you have been disappointed or hold an unmet expectation. As you are aware of this feeling of your needs being unmet, recognize that there is a sense of incompleteness in you. As you are aware of this experience, without judging yourself, come fully to the refuge. Bring awareness to the unbounded space of being, listen to the inner silence, and feel the richness and completeness of the moment. Rest here, allowing the sensations and feelings of your unmet needs to be hosted in the liveliness of the connection to spaciousness. As they are hosted fully, they gradually dissolve. As they dissolve, you connect with the liveliness and fullness that are naturally present in this moment. In this way, you experience the power to go beyond conflict-producing hopes. Recognize, understand, and rest in the second refuge, feel nourished in so doing, and imagine radiating this sense of vitality to the other person, allowing the other to be as they are.

The Gift of Warmth: The Body of Great Bliss

With the third refuge we speak of warmth. The body of great bliss is a sense of natural warmth that arises from open awareness. You are open and you are aware of the openness. This awareness of openness is referred to as *union,* and this union spontaneously births warmth and positive qualities. You are connected and feel the warmth of being who you are. Now is the time to manifest and to engage others. You will discover that humor will spontaneously come from the confidence and awareness you have. If there is no self-confidence, there can be no genuine playfulness and humor. Humor comes from playfulness, playfulness comes from warmth, warmth comes from confidence, and confidence comes from openness.

With the gift of warmth, you are able to dance with someone as they discover their creativity. Your actions don't interfere. As we experience the gift of space and awareness and warmth, we want to fully allow and participate with others. Share. Merge. Move. Sing. Laugh. Accomplish. This is a beautiful experience to achieve in one's life. There is nothing greater than finding space, awareness, and warmth in you, and engaging with that warmth and sharing it with others.

Overcoming Suffering with the Third Refuge

The warmth of inner bliss melts the frozen structures of suffering and pain. It frees us from inner ignorance; it heals pain, sickness, blockages, and troubled relationships. The warmth that arises from the connection of awareness and openness is the greatest medicine, the greatest healer within us.

In your meditation practice you can work with experiences of discomfort, pain, or sickness. Bring open and clear attention to your pain or sickness, and feel pervasive space, because it is already there. It is not that you are bringing space to your pain; rather, you are becoming aware of the presence of spaciousness and connecting to it. This means that you do not reject your pain in any way, nor do you elaborate upon it by thinking or talking to yourself. The moment you feel the space in the presence of your illness or pain, you can feel the light of awareness, the connection, the warmth, and you begin to heal. You allow spontaneous healing, for as you recognize the space that is already there, the warmth of connection manifests spontaneously.

Continue resting the warmth of your attention in the area of your discomfort. As you are aware and feel that warmth, gradually bring your attention right into the center of the pain, the blockage, or the sickness. The more spaciousness and openness you feel, the more your natural ability to heal is supported.

Unbounded space is a great gift, infinite awareness is a great gift, and natural and spontaneous warmth is a great gift. These gifts are already in us in this very moment. As you recognize this, you come to *know* this. This knowing becomes the greatest resource in your life. This knowing is what has been lacking. We have lacked the conscious recognition of what is inherently here within us. In this moment, you can become conscious of this great gift of warmth. Many experiences arise from that warmth, such as joy, love, compassion, kindness, care, acknowledgment, appreciation, enthusiasm, and devotion. All the qualities that arise from that warmth are gifts.

It is not necessary to strategize and plan to express the gifts of warmth. Our inner intelligence knows when and where and to whom to manifest specific qualities. This intelligence knows far more than any ego will know. Trust this. When the right moment comes, you will remember; you will know what to do and how to give. You will naturally and spontaneously give to those who are in pain, suffering, sick, and lost. You will open to those who are confused, hostile, aggressive, and mean from pain and confusion. Many suffer and need your gifts. Be aware that you have gifts to give. As you discover that you are the gift, you discover that giving is more joyful than receiving.

You may wish to deepen your experience of the inner refuge by listening to Track 3 of the CD, Guided Meditation: Inner Refuge.

CHAPTER FOUR

VISION IS MIND

Having explored the power of drawing our attention within and discovering the gifts of the inner refuge, we are ready to receive the heart instructions of Dawa Gyaltsen, the concise guidance he offers that can lead us from conflict and confusion to freedom. As we explore and contemplate the meaning of each line, may you discover how this ancient teaching can be a remedy for any confusion and suffering you experience. Here are the five lines, the quintessential teachings of this highly revered meditation master from my tradition:

Vision is mind.
Mind is empty.
Emptiness is clear light.
Clear light is union.
Union is great bliss.

"Vision" encompasses two fundamental things: the subject or self, and the objects or appearances formed by the imagination of that self. Both are equally unreal and are certainly not as solid and concrete as we see and feel them to be. When you say, "I am feeling sad," or "I am feeling hurt," that "I" is formed by the imagination.

It is not inherently real. I have referred to this sense of "I" as the pain body. If you look closely at that "I" or ego, is it really there? Does it solidly exist? Many meditation masters have sent their students on journeys of inquiry to investigate this "I." Does it have a shape or color? Is it thick or thin? Is it located inside the body or outside the body? Can you actually find it? When you thoroughly and exhaustively investigate the apparent solidity of this "I," it is not possible to conclude that there is anything inherently there. It is amazing that something that doesn't inherently exist can produce so much pain, create so many complex stories, and need such elaborate defenses. But that is what happens when we fail to recognize the truth that there is no solidly existing self. Recognizing that the self does not inherently exist is the beginning of the cessation of suffering.

Ego survives and thrives through the imagination. Appearances and stories are the food of ego. If those appearances "dissolve" one after another, if we recognize that they are not as solid as they appear, ego gets weaker and weaker and weaker. So to understand the first line of Dawa Gyaltsen's teaching, *Vision is mind,* we bring our attention to the appearances created by ego. We start with what appears in our life, because that is a place where we are more obviously caught.

What is an example of a typical "vision" that expresses or captures our suffering in any given moment? We may find ourselves feeling or thinking:

That person is really annoying me.
This is a waste of time.
I wish he would leave me alone.
I hope she contacts me.
I don't know what's wrong with me.

How am I going to pay this bill?
I just don't have the energy to do that.
I'm so jumpy I can't stand this.
This is boring.
I hope I get that job.

According to Dawa Gyaltsen, all of the above statements and their accompanying scenarios are created by the imagination of ego. Yet when something "appears" in this way, it often seems real and true. We believe we need to do something about it, or we feel powerless to do anything about it, or we try to ignore and distract ourselves from feeling something about it. You may say, "Well, it is obvious that many things are just the imagination of ego, but some of my problems are real. My mother is dying and that is not my imagination." *Vision is mind* is not saying that your mother is not dying, but if you realize the truth that *Vision is mind* points to, your relation to your dying mother can be one of beauty and compassion. Perhaps we have begun to meditate, and we think, *Oh, I can just be with that. I can accommodate that suffering. I know: like all things, it will pass.* Even that is missing the opportunity that *Vision is mind* points to. There is a more direct and vital relationship to our life's experiences, to the appearances of mind, that we can have.

In everyday life, when you really like someone or something, or when you become angry or disappointed by someone, where is your attachment or your aversion directed? To the object. The object becomes the focus. "Who" is liking or disliking is not so obvious or important to us, because we are focused on the object. We can so easily become fixated or focused on appearances that we disconnect from ourselves. We may not be conscious of what is happening in ourselves; instead, we locate our experience out there in the other person. It is that particular person that I love or hate.

There may have been a progression or development that preceded this conclusion, but we are no longer aware of it. With aversion, for example, you may dislike what a person did or said. *I really don't like it when you do that.* That experience goes on for some time and finally you just think, *I don't like you. It really doesn't matter what you do at this point because I just don't like you.* When you create this imagination of ego, there is an unsettled, ungrounded, vulnerable place in you that projects the cause of this insecurity as having to do with what some other person is doing or saying. So you attack, criticize, or otherwise seek to change that person. If it goes on long enough, you just conclude that the other person is bad or wrong or dangerous. Ego has clearly created a solid vision, and you are stuck with that vision.

If you do any kind of personal work that involves reflection, you begin to shift your focus from the object or other person, to the subject or the one who is distressed. People who don't work with themselves at all just see their projection as the full story. Those who work more with themselves find some kind of space to reflect more upon themselves: *What am I feeling? Why am I angry?* So your awareness begins to shift from the person or situation to yourself. In spiritual practice, awareness is always 100 percent focused upon oneself. In the end you conquer the demon of ignorance in yourself, not the demon that is the projection of ignorance. The outer demon is not the source of your problem; it is only an appearance coming from the source within. And in deep spiritual work, you are interested in cutting the root of suffering and confusion, not just cutting off a branch, for there will always be another branch.

So first we must understand *Vision is mind.* The only way the apparent solidity of your vision can dissolve is when you recognize its nature, its condition. The only way to recognize this is to look back to who has produced it. Where do we begin? It is important to begin where we are, in the state in which we find ourselves.

In helping students recognize their own personal experiences, I use the term "famous person" or "famous situation." By "famous" I am referring to your perception, whether momentary or prolonged, that a person or situation appears in your life as a problem. If it is a person, you may feel this person knows which button to press to make you feel uncomfortable. You may recognize you are experiencing a "famous person" after you have avoided returning someone's phone calls for several days, or you find yourself arguing with this person in your vivid imagination as you take your morning shower. You can be sure that you are imagining your famous person, for even simple logic shows that the person is the loving mother or brother or a good friend of someone else. This person may be good things to others, but for you is an annoyance or problem. Such is the vision created by the imagination of ego. An example of a "famous situation" could be anxiety and dread over giving a presentation at work, or finding that you are always late for appointments.

Whatever it is for you at this time, examine this problem in your own mind. Is it really as solid and concrete as you are experiencing it to be? Can this situation exist in the way that it does without depending on its subject (you)? How is it possible to realize that it is not truly there in the way that you are experiencing it? It is important to look closely—nakedly and directly—at how this person or situation lives in you. Bring your focus inward. If you keep your focus steadily and directly on the experience of the famous person or situation as it lives in you, you will find many thoughts and sensations and movements of the mind. Be still; listen to the silence; recognize the spaciousness, and continue to host the experience. What do you discover? You will find the experience cannot maintain itself unless you continue to participate in its creation. If you look closely, as you connect with stillness, silence, and spaciousness, it is possible to become free from the object of ego, free from your famous person or situation, free from your vision. That freedom is the goal expressed by this line *Vision is mind*.

GUIDED MEDITATION PRACTICE OF *VISION IS MIND*

At this point in your reading, you may wish to work with the guided meditation on the CD accompanying this book, or you may follow the guidance that follows to support you in recognizing that *Vision is mind*.

Sit in a comfortable posture. Draw your attention inward. Feel stillness in your body, silence in your speech, and spaciousness in your mind. Just feel stillness, silence, and spaciousness while you feel connected and present in your body. Allow time for this.

Now invite whatever is bothering you to come to awareness. You may be experiencing a "famous person" who is an object of your fear, aversion, or desire, or there may be a particular situation that is bothering you or blocking the creative flow of your life. As you rest, look at that object formed by your egoistic imagination.

As you bring your vision to mind, you may become aware of many thoughts, or an internal dialogue, or uncomfortable feelings or sensations in your body. Simply say *Vision is mind* to yourself three times to remind yourself of the practice. Look at the vision internally. Look with open awareness—simple, direct, and clear observation. Look nakedly. Look closer and closer. Don't look with another pain, another thought. Don't talk with another voice. Just use nonconceptual, direct observation. In this way you are hosting the appearance in the refuge space without further elaboration through thinking or analysis.

Observe nakedly whatever image is present, without concepts, thoughts, or judgments. Just see it. Whatever sensations or feelings are present, simply experience them. Look with open, naked awareness. This is seeing with the wisdom eye.

As you do that, magic happens. The conversation and imagination of ego, the fantasies of ego, stop. You are no longer feeding them or engaging with them. You simply hold the vision that ego has created in pure, open awareness. When you truly see with the wisdom eye, there is nothing solid that can sustain itself. Whatever you experience dissipates. The colors, shapes, or characteristics of your experience dissolve; the image of your famous person or situation dissipates; negativity releases and you cease to feel that anything substantial is there. It is as if you are looking at a slide projected on a wall, and as you walk toward it, getting closer and closer, whatever image you saw from a distance, you can no longer perceive when you are up close. Nothing remains. There is no discrete image; there is only light. That is the realization of the first line: *Vision is mind.* You are free from the imagination of ego. You feel some sense of release.

Only mind remains; the object is no longer there. Therefore, we say, *Vision is mind.* When you look at that vision with that open eye of naked awareness, there is no solid object out there or in here. Simply become the one who is seeing, which is the mind itself.

See nakedly. Observe directly. Rest in open awareness. Trust this experience.

Realizing *Vision is mind* is a very powerful experience. Something you have experienced as solidly existing, creating a problem, or otherwise blocking your creativity, is not substantial. Recognizing this is very simple, and yet it is often difficult to trust the experience. It is simple if you look nakedly and very difficult if you look with a "smart ego."

When There Is No Obvious Challenge

What if you cannot think of a "famous person" or a specific challenging situation in your life to look at in the meditation? In that case, you may bring your attention to whatever you perceive at this very moment. Perhaps you are aware of sunlight and space and colors and sounds and the feeling of people around you. All that comes to your senses, your sense consciousness, and sense objects are also "vision." Perhaps you are having very subtle experiences in relation to your perceptions, but you are not conscious of them. Can you see and feel everything around you while experiencing a deep stillness? If so, that is also what *Vision is mind* means. All these visions *are* my mind, and I experience them as such. Meditation begins there. It is not necessary to go out of your way to think about some issues or choose some pain in your life in order to realize *Vision is mind*. But when the pain body is strongly present in your life, something has chosen you. So bring your awareness to what you experience at this very moment. Your experience of your pain body may not be as luminous as the sun or as clear as the cloudless sky or as pleasurable as the feeling of being surrounded by fellow meditators. The pain body does not have that light and luminous quality, but nonetheless, it is your vision. The only way to overcome it is to be conscious of it.

We may know conceptually that things are not as they appear, but we feel this vision's presence so strongly that it is disturbing.

The whole approach of the practice when we say *Vision is mind* is to look at that object, that vision, which is the imagination of ego. It is very important not to look at that object which I am referring to as the pain body with the eyes of ego. That is a common mistake you can make in this practice. If that happens, it doesn't change anything. You are not realizing *Vision is mind*. It is just another layer of ego. Another pain is looking at the pain. *Why me? Why now? Why am I still feeling this way? What's wrong with me?* There is a desperate sense of ego looking at the pain, and you experience effort and fear and restlessness—so many mixed emotions. Looking in this way is not going to clear your suffering for sure, and will only create more discomfort. Or we look with the smarter ego: *Oh, I can see that this pain is just my grasping mind. So I'm going to breathe out and let go. I'm letting go now.* Whether we look at pain with obvious pain, or look at pain with a smarter ego, we are not realizing *Vision is mind.* So it is important to look nakedly and directly, with the wisdom eye, or openness. Knowing how to experience and apply that in the practice of meditation is key.

Let's say you are looking at sense objects and experiences, which are also vision. When there is no particular pain you are facing, you simply look directly at sense experience. Feel the space. It is important to perceive sensory experience and feel the space. When you are meditating according to *dzogchen*, you allow your eyes to remain open. When your eyes are open, you perceive many things, and this can be distracting for some people. Can you be aware of the existence of colorful shapes and sensations, and thoughts and feelings and emotions, in the space of open awareness? If you develop the ability to do so, perhaps you can host your pain with openness. Hosting sensory experience in awareness can be likened to the sky hosting a rainbow. Emotional pain is more like the waves of the ocean, which may appear harder to host in awareness because of the greater movement. But as you become familiar with hosting thoughts and sensations in open awareness, it will become easier to host stronger movements of mind. However, if you are not used to hosting anything, it will be hard to host pain. The hardest is to host your reaction to the challenging object, the famous person, or the famous or challenging situation. Because they appear so convincingly threatening, your own thoughts and feelings and sensations in reaction to them are difficult to host.

In the ordinary moments of everyday life, it is important to be aware of space. When there is no obvious challenge or threat, the seemingly mundane moments are excellent times to become aware of the space of being. But actually, we usually try to be aware of space when it is more difficult, because our need or sense of urgency is greater. When everything is okay, we just have fun in samsara. We can wait for luminosity because things are fine. But when challenged by pain and confusion, we start to look for relief, for light, for joy. There may be times when you can simply close your eyes and feel the presence of joy in your heart. And there are times when, able to experience the presence of joy, you may see the possibility of expanding and pervading and manifesting that joy through action and creativity. But there are many people who close their eyes and feel nothing at all, or feel pain. So there are two categories of experience: times where you feel openness directly, and times where you feel blocked or in pain. When are you more likely to turn toward meditation? When you are in pain. Why is this so? When you are feeling no obvious pain, it is easy to think, *I don't need to do this practice. I'm fine.* But if you think this way, a deeper joy is hidden from you. You don't reach this deeper joy, because you don't go far enough. It is the right time to meditate when you do have joy in your life. Meditation supports the ripening and expansion of positive qualities and actions.

At moments when you do experience pain and suffering, you might turn to meditation to feel relief, but find you are unable to do so because you are trying too hard. You may feel more obscured and more blocked, and the world around you may appear harsh and overwhelming. This can increase a sense of desperation. Seeking, needing, and trying hard to find relief, it may not occur to you to try less, to open more, to feel more, and to be aware more fully. First of all, we are afraid that if we open more when we feel pain, it means that we will feel more pain. We forget that the instruction is to open and *bring attention to the openness itself.* It is important to realize that the mind that is able to be more aware is not the mind that is trying harder. How do I find the open mind? Only with less effort. When I relax effort and resistance, I can find the mind that is there, just present. When you feel through that open mind and see through that open mind with effortless awareness, you will experience the dissolution of the pain body. Only through effortlessness can the clouds of the effortful conceptual mind dissipate. If you have a deeper sense of trust, you will put less effort into resisting pain or creating some alternative state of mind. You will glimpse the openness of mind that is actually present and is the true refuge.

So close your eyes and see that famous person, famous situation, or yourself, the famous meditator who is struggling in this moment. Feel exactly the way you are experiencing this moment. Just be with that. Most important is the way you look at or observe the appearance, the object of your egoistic imagination: Observe directly with naked, pure awareness. Feel the experience intimately, without resisting or maintaining any distance or perspective. Come energetically closer to whatever sensations or feelings you experience. Allow your experience fully and openly. As you do that, awareness is like the sun's warmth, and the object formed by egoistic imagination is like frost. The moment sunlight touches that frost, it begins to melt and become liquid. Naked awareness is sunshine, warmth, and when that object dissolves, you will feel the energy in your body becoming looser and opening up and flowing. As this happens, your mind becomes clearer. You experience space within—new and fresh and alive in your body and mind and energy field. The key is not to look at your experience through egoistic imagination or elaboration, but experience it directly as it is and as it dissolves. What remains is openness, and the awareness of openness itself.

Many times students have told me, "I was trying to do that, but it became more painful." That means you are looking through another painful egoistic imagination. Anytime you are experiencing more pain, awareness is not naked or pure. You are experiencing another layer of ego having a subtle communication and dialogue with pain. Nothing has changed. It is most important to recognize deep stillness, silence, and spaciousness as you encounter the challenge.

As we mentioned before, pain is an important doorway to inner refuge. When you are challenged in your life and facing difficulty, don't run away. You have a great tool to work with pain, a great wisdom eye to look directly; you have an amazing method to deal with suffering. *Vision is mind* is our encouragement to not run away. Your pain can be transformed to bliss. *Vision is mind* is support to encounter the pain body. When you experience the pain body, *Vision is mind* motivates you. You need the protection and support of refuge, and if you use the practice as support, pain transforms to bliss. Pain becomes the true doorway. Without pain, realization might be difficult. There is subtle pain we don't even recognize as pain, and in fact we call it pleasure. And often with pleasure, we feel we don't have to look for anything. Self-realization will not occur, because you simply don't see the need.

When we identify with the object of bliss or samsaric joy, we don't think there is a problem. I love pizza. There is no problem. I love chocolate. There is no problem. But when I feel pain because I am not allowed to eat pizza anymore or I become allergic to chocolate, then I'm looking for a remedy. So pain brings you into the search for a solution. And when you wonder how you can understand the ego, it is especially obvious when you are in pain. *I feel pain. I am sad. I am depressed.* The ego who is suffering is easier to recognize than the one for whom suffering is not that intense. So in some sense, there is more advantage when you are suffering in an obvious way.

If the eye that perceives the vision is another pain body, *Vision is mind* cannot be realized. If it is naked awareness, then it is realized. What is difficult for us is that we have a strong, long habit of being in our pain body and looking at the world through our habits, through the eyes of the pain body. The practice of naked observation is simple, but our habits are strong and complex. One common reflex when experiencing pain is to separate from the pain and put distance between yourself and the pain. What we don't recognize is that the distance is the problem. Distance is produced by our fear of an experience. And as long as we remain distant, we will never be free of pain and the fear of pain. So it is important to locate that person, situation, object, or experience that is challenging or difficult, and recognize it as your vision. Usually we engage our vision by thinking and strategizing and speculating and talking to ourselves and others. That is how we habitually engage. We try to get a handle on things. With *Vision is mind*, in order to liberate suffering, we don't want to do what we usually do. We don't want to see with the deluded eye; we want to engage the wisdom eye. That is the only way it will change. So we need to observe directly, observe nakedly, observe without thinking, observe without distancing, being intimate in our practice, and not separating ourselves from our experience.

What is the benefit of realizing *Vision is mind*? As an example, at this moment I am looking at the cup of tea that is next to me. This is quite a lovely cup that one of my students gave to me. If I have attachment to this cup, I cannot experience myself clearly, because I am looking at the world—in this case, my cup—from a place of attachment. If I am aware of that, conscious of my attachment, that allows me to let go and relax and feel more open. I'm still looking at the cup. But now I'm seeing the cup from openness. This is an ordinary example, but such a moment in our lives is unexamined, and therefore unrecognized as an opportunity to fully enter the natural state of mind. Seeing clearly in this way for even 30 seconds will have an impact on how I relate to myself and the world as I experience it. Because of this simple release of attachment, I am experiencing a new relationship.

Of course, when you are suffering and you look at the object of your attachment, if you look back to the subject, you, the one who is suffering, you can see loneliness, need, and fear. That is who you are identifying with, but it is not who you are. The only way to understand that this is not who you are is to be conscious. As you are aware of the one who is lonely, as you host the experience in open awareness, you will feel the release of that pain. Deep inside is the fear that if you lose what you have, something will happen to you. When you feel that fear while experiencing inner stillness, the power of experiencing the inner stillness releases the pain body of insecurity. That stillness is indestructible. That is a fundamental and perceivable quality of space—ceaseless, changeless, deathless, and birthless. These qualities are not perceivable by the ego; they are perceivable only with naked awareness, the wisdom eye. These are the fundamental qualities of space, and perceiving them affects our state of mind. We feel the indestructible quality. You feel, *I am not dependent on the other person's approval or attention,* because in the stillness itself the survival mind is not dominating your experience. That is why the recognition of that stillness is the clear, direct antidote of fear. Fear is fundamentally the fear of change. Connecting with stillness is a direct experience of the changeless space of being. That is why it is a direct antidote. You discover the connection to the changeless space of being and immediately feel released from the pain body, which is the fear of change. It is natural.

When you rest deeply in that quality of changelessness, you are free from attachment to any outcome. If this person does this, it is fine; if this person doesn't do that, it is fine. How does such confidence develop? It ripens by being in the changeless space longer. That is all. Just trust and remain longer, and confidence will emerge by itself. That sense of well-being comes naturally when one is more familiar with the practice of abiding in openness.

THE INFORMAL PRACTICE OF *VISION IS MIND*

How do you work with your everyday experiences? Connecting with the inner refuge of stillness, silence, and spaciousness brings the medicine of *Vision is mind* into everyday life. So the informal practice is to take the three pills of stillness, silence, and spaciousness that we discussed in Chapter 1.

In everyday life, vision appears. Suppose your boss is your "famous person," and you go to the office and actually see your boss on a daily basis. Now your boss not only appears in your imagination, but you also hear and see and receive e-mails and directives from this person. Throughout your day, whenever you feel yourself hemmed in by conditions and limitations, and experience tension, discomfort, anger, sadness, or other emotions, simply hold the space of stillness. Just draw your attention to your body, be with whatever you are feeling, and feel the stillness of the body. Check in: *Am I feeling stillness?* Then continue with your day, doing whatever you need to do while maintaining a connection to that stillness. If you do this, you will feel protected within the situation and from your own overwhelming emotions. The moment you draw attention to stillness, you will begin to feel that protection and support. Stillness is the medicine for the pain body.

Second, if your life involves much energy around conversation and dialogue; much internal arguing and mentally talking to yourself; or bickering or gossip in the work environment, draw your attention inward and listen to the silence. Ask yourself, *Am I hearing silence? Am I feeling the silence? Am I being in that silence? Am I silence? . . . I hear it. I feel it. I am it.* The moment you feel you *are* that silence, you are free from the voices within you and the voices of others around you. You are free from the critical voices of yourself and your boss. It doesn't mean you don't listen to your boss! It means you don't listen from a fearful, agitated, and angry place. You listen from deep silence. You hear more and communicate more from that creative and wise silence. Silence is the medicine for pain speech.

The spaciousness of awareness is the medicine for the pain mind. Perhaps at some point in your day you are angry or jealous or feel overwhelmed. At that moment you don't feel any spaciousness. You are occupied with anger or a sense of loss or depression. The pain mind has manifested and occupied your space. But you can rediscover that space. How? Simply by being open and allowing whatever emotions you are experiencing. Don't push down anger. Don't invite further anger. Don't negotiate with anger. Host the anger and simply feel the space within and around the anger. With awareness, you can journey to the center of the experience of anger by being open to it and feeling the space in and around it. That spaciousness is the medicine of the pain mind.

In Conclusion: *Vision Is Mind*

With *Vision is mind*, I have been instructing you to directly and nakedly experience whatever you are experiencing. I humorously refer to the famous person, the famous situation, the famous moment—whatever that is for you—and encourage you to bring your attention to that experience. Whatever is bothering you or whatever you are experiencing is an image or appearance or occurrence formed by the imagination of ego. Again, the important point is *how* you look at your experience. The instruction is to observe directly, nonconceptually, nakedly. These are the words used.

When I am looking directly at my experience, I'm not trying to interpret what I'm doing by saying that object or that experience is necessary or not necessary. Do not further engage the commenting mind. Be still in your body, and still in your internal energy, and just look at your experience. This is one way to understand how to observe. Another way to phrase it is *Just be aware.* It is the same outcome as far as realization is concerned. In *dzogchen* there is an expression: *nakedly observing, nakedly liberating.* "Observing" here means experiencing with awareness. Can you gaze at a flower without judging and without thoughts? Can you see the flower clearly and vividly, without commentary? A flower is outside you, while anger is experienced as inside, but both are called "vision" because the process is the same: gaze upon your anger without thought, directly with awareness. Sometimes you may be looking at an image that you associate with anger, such as the face of your boss, and at other times you bring attention to your angry feeling itself when it is present in the moment. You can be aware of the anger itself, rather than always interpreting anger, or being driven into thinking fueled by anger. *Vision is mind.*

Observe the object formed by the imagination of ego. You can observe the fear of death, or the fear of not being productive or not accomplishing anything. Any fear that you are aware of, observe it nakedly. Usually we spin so many stories when we feel something such as anger or fear. *I hate that feeling of fear.* Or we change the words as we talk to ourselves: *Oh, it is not death I'm afraid of, it is living.* So we change the words and we read more books to see if someone has a better spin on our suffering, and we get busy rear-ranging our thinking about our problem. What we don't do is let it be as it is. Observe nakedly, look nakedly, nonconceptually. Simply put: be aware of it. *Vision is mind.*

As you are aware for longer and longer periods of time, eventually anger just clears. It is very surprising and pleasurable. But then you may hear yourself thinking: *I'm faking it; I must be avoiding the real issue.* Those thoughts and words can be quite vivid. But the truth is, in order for ego to survive, it needs its object. A subject without an object cannot survive while remaining what it is. If there is no pain or conflict, ego cannot survive in its habitual form. That is why you hear your inner voice say, *I'm just making this up and avoiding the real issue because I can't face it.* That is why it is important to continue listening to the silence. Hear the silence. The power of this practice is to continuously remain aware, simply be aware of that object. As you do so, all the clouds disappear.

When that happens, what you are experiencing is the mind itself. You begin to feel the luminous aspect of the mind. You begin to feel the one who is looking. Only the mind is there. There is no solid object there. Only the mind is there, the one who is seeing it.

You realize this by simply being conscious of it, rather than feasting on the food of words and thoughts about the object. *Vision is mind.* When you are simply and directly and nakedly aware, the object dissolves, and what remains is quite luminous because mind is luminous. When you are conscious of it, that distressing object is nothing more than the clear, luminous presence of mind. Making this discovery is wonderful medicine.

Now you are ready for the next investigation: what is mind?

CHAPTER FIVE

MIND IS EMPTY

I had the opportunity at the age of 26 to leave my monastery in India and travel throughout Tibet. I was invited to teach in a small monastery. I was reluctant to teach, since I was only 26 years old, and the monks who requested the teaching were as old as 70. But they were persistent in their request, and so I accepted. The older monks took the occasion very seriously. First they invited all the villagers into the shrine room of the monastery to partake in a purification ritual. At the conclusion of the ritual, they sent the villagers out. They then posted guards outside the monastery doors, and only the older monks were present for my teaching. I asked them to share their practice experiences and understanding. Gradually, one after another, each monk opened up and shared. On the basis of what I heard from each, I responded. As we finished, an older monk with one blind eye took me to the back of the meditation hall. As he held my hand, he told me that he had received the introduction to the nature of mind from the successor to Shardza Tashi Gyaltsen—a realized master who was revered throughout Tibet—but went on to say that he didn't get to clarify the instruction before the many changes happened in Tibet, during which time his master died. Therefore, some doubt had remained in his mind. As tears streamed down his face he thanked me for my teaching, saying, "You have cleared my doubt. For the rest of my life, I know how to practice."

For this elderly monk, my words had pointed to a very specific place within him that was beyond doubt. He recognized this nature of mind in himself and became clear. And now, for the remainder of his life, he understood that his practice was to abide and connect again and again in this nature of mind, until he had completely integrated this understanding throughout all of his experiences, whether waking or sleeping, sitting or lying down. As this monk expressed, the understanding of the nature of mind is highly treasured.

Historically, when a student set off in search of a teacher from the lineage of the Zhang Zhung Nyen Gyü, their aim was to receive the instructions of the nature of mind. They were looking to be introduced to this very simple place within themselves. This introduction is referred to as *ngo trö*, often translated as "pointing-out instructions," though it literally means "being shown your own face." The master's role is to show you your own face, or introduce you to yourself. And that means that place, that clear and open space of mind, which is your own face. This is the nature of mind. That whole process and understanding is very, very important, more than this or that breathing exercise, or this or that movement technique. None are as important as the recognition of this core place. This nature of mind is where the poem of inner refuge and the instructions of Dawa Gyaltsen point us.

GETTING TO KNOW YOURSELF

I was speaking to a Western friend of mine who also was a meditation practitioner of many years. He said, "I'm finally beginning to know myself." I was curious. "What do you mean?" I asked him. He replied, "After being in a relationship for twelve years, my partner and I finally decided to go our separate ways. Now I have been in a new relationship for a few months, and I am finding that I am experiencing so much jealousy! I never knew I was such a jealous person. It is a real eye-opening experience to discover this about myself." As I listened, I found it curious that someone would feel that he was getting to know himself as he was getting in touch and more familiar with his pain body. How could he think this was getting to know himself? I realize that this is often what people mean when they speak about getting to know themselves. They are speaking about becoming more familiar with their suffering or their pain body. What that tells me is that the core message and medicine of Dawa Gyaltsen's line *Mind is empty* is not commonly appreciated or understood. Don't get too excited if your final realization about yourself is that you are a jealous person. You are concluding in the wrong place. You have to go further and look deeper to get to the truth of that pain body, that pain identity. Is the pain body truly there? No. It is not there in the way that it appears. If you look directly and intimately without the interference of the conceptual mind, you will discover that the pain body does not inherently exist. Realizing this is freedom. Why is it that we so easily feel we have uncovered a truer self when we say, "I realize I am a jealous person!" We haven't recognized the one who is realizing this. We have not looked directly at the one who has come to this conclusion. If you can be conscious of *that* ego, both the subject and the object will dissolve. When you feel the dissolution of that subject, then if you want to, you can say that you are beginning to know yourself. You are beginning to know your *true* self: boundless and indestructible.

So I am touching upon a big topic here. Of course, I am presenting the pain body in a simplified way, and it is important to have respect for that conventional self because that is the doorway to your transformation. Although you are not your pain body, often the healing of the misunderstanding that you are your pain begins when you connect more deeply with your pain body, just like the meditator who connected with his jealousy. It can be a moving experience that you want to share with others, and even though that is not conclusively who you truly are, it can be the first step toward healing. Often we do not allow ourselves to know our pain very well, or to feel it fully. We may feel some cultural pressure to be successful and uplifted and energetic. You are supposed to feel happy. But are you really happy? Everyone else seems excited about something, and so you smile and jump up and down and join a conspiracy of happiness. If that is the case, discovering your pain body can be more authentic than joining a conspiracy of cheerfulness that takes you further away from yourself. Again, Dawa Gyaltsen is directing us to look even more nakedly. Pain is your doorway or entrance to a deeper realization, so let's continue to explore how that happens.

Dawa Gyaltsen's second line of advice is *Mind is empty*. What do we mean by *mind,* and what does *empty* refer to? The mind is the one who has created or formed the egoistic imagination, the vision. Mind is the creator of all the stories. Usually we don't experience mind as clear or open or empty or uncontrived, for we are more focused on what is occupying the mind—the experience or the story. We don't realize that when it is filled with obscurations, mind is limited and contracted and blocked; therefore, it is important to discover the experience that mind is empty and clear and open and luminous. That is the goal of the practice in this second line.

Through the advice of the first line of Dawa Gyaltsen, *Vision is mind*, we realize there is nothing that appears in our experience that is fixed or solid. Whatever you experience, it is just your own mind. What is that mind? The way to find out is not to question intellectually or to analyze or judge or think, but to discover through nonconceptual awareness: naked awareness, openness, direct observation. Now you look inward toward the subject, rather than outward toward the object as we did in our first investigation of looking at vision. As you direct your focus inward ask yourself: What is mind? What does it look like? Does it have any shape or color, or is it located in a particular place? Close your eyes and go closer and closer with open, naked awareness. As you get close, the mind also dissipates. It dissolves its solidity or concreteness, and whatever block, fear, or negative emotion it encounters, such as anger or jealousy, simply dissolves. How is this possible? It dissolves because it cannot sustain itself without the imagination or the continued conversation of ego. When you nakedly observe, you are not talking or commenting from the smart ego's perspective. As you look nakedly with open awareness, what you observe dissolves. You actually experience that it dissolves into vast space. Nothing remains. We use the word *emptiness* for that experience. *Mind is empty.* It is clear. So as a result of the practice, you feel a deep release of that pain, that emotion, that block.

When you recognize *Vision is mind*, you feel a deep release. What you thought really existed, the object, is simply not there in the way that you experienced it. Fifty percent is gone because you realize *Vision is mind;* and with the second line, *Mind is empty,* what you think of as "me" or "I," the subject, does not remain as well. The other half dissolves. As a result, you feel enormous inner freedom and release.

But what is tricky—particularly for those not used to looking at mind—is that another ego may be looking. Instead of looking from an open place, you may be looking through the eyes of a smart ego. Rather than observing from the place of deep silence, there is a conversation, a voice that feels subtler and wiser, but it is still the voice of the ego. That way of looking at your mind does not enable you to find the spacious quality around and within it; you are still looking at mind with a sense of limit and condition. You look at your mind, but the one who is looking is not that sense of spaciousness. At this point it is helpful to bring awareness to the observer, rather than to the object. What supports you to be more nakedly aware of the observer? Three words: stillness, silence, spaciousness. Feel stillness in your body; hear the silence within; recognize the spaciousness of mind, and look at that mind. Mind immediately feels empty. That is what is meant by *Mind is empty.*

The benefit of this practice is that you feel release. *I am not this pain. I am not this conflict. I am clear; I am open.* That openness is called emptiness. *Mind is empty.*

What is the mind that Dawa Gyaltsen describes as empty? It is ego. It is useful to describe ego in three ways: pain body, pain speech, and the pain mind, for we experience suffering through these three doors. Each of these is empty. All three are that mind, and that *Mind is empty.* You understand *Mind is empty* when the mind is free of the pain body, pain voice, and the pain mind. *Empty* means clear, open, and free. So it becomes possible to realize the bliss body, bliss speech, and bliss mind through the practice.

The theoretical and philosophical definition of emptiness is "the lack of inherent existence." Here we are not talking intellectually but experientially. That means one's own ego is the producer of the pain body, pain speech, and the pain mind, and when we realize that not only is the imagination of ego illusory, but ego itself is not there as we thought it was, we become clear and free.

To realize *Vision is mind* and *Mind is empty,* it is necessary to observe pain body, pain speech, and the pain mind in a particular way. That is key. That observing mind is naked awareness, being conscious of that pain body, being conscious of that pain voice, being conscious of that pain mind. You might say, "Oh, I know I have a pain body, pain speech, pain mind." That knowing doesn't liberate anything. That is a thought. That is conceptual knowing, not naked knowing. The definition of *naked* is "without clothes," so naked knowing is without the clothing of concepts and thoughts. What is left when the concepts and thoughts are not obscuring the mind? Pure awareness. In *dzogchen* that awareness is referred to as *rigpa*. It is the Tibetan word for innate awareness, being conscious of spaciousness itself. This awareness doesn't come from outside; in fact, it is neither outside nor inside, but awareness itself.

Knowing is not an observer looking at ego from outside or inside. The mind that is the observer is still the ego. The only way to exhaust the ego chain is to be nakedly aware. The observing ego thinks this is the last and the most beautiful unknown ego. Even if this ego is "ego" in small golden letters with rainbow light around it, nonetheless it is ego. Ego cannot witness its own funeral. Effort dissolves into the vast space of pure, naked awareness. It is aware in itself. When you look directly at "the one who is observing," the observing mind releases into the vast and luminous space. So look at the subject instead of trying to be aware of the object of the ego. Be aware of the one who is bothered. Be aware of the one who is fearful. Be aware of the one who is feeling uncomfortable. And be aware of the one who is aware. When that knowing, *rigpa*, or naked awareness, sees pain body, pain speech, and the pain mind, suffering is liberated. Liberation comes through the power of that naked, open awareness. Again, this awareness is not conceptual. If you are looking at your painful mind and it doesn't become blissful mind, you are not looking with the right mind. You have to be aware of the one who is observing. It is less important to know *what* you are observing and more important to connect with the right observer. *Who* is observing rather than *what* is being observed is the key.

To express this in another way, we have explored coming to the realization of *Vision is mind* through working with the example of the famous person. When you look nakedly at the solid famous person out there, you do not find something solid. Instead, what you do find is a solid, famous hidden you. You become the hidden famous person yourself. You frequently see and notice that suffering is in your mind and thoughts and dreams and subconscious stirrings. When you feel through the practice that the cause of your suffering is no longer "out there" as you have previously felt it to be, *you* become more present. So now you need to continue on an inner journey to investigate whether that you, that ego, is solid. Your ego is the famous person. Who is this famous spinner of stories? If you come up with an answer, keep looking.

Guided Meditation Practice of *Mind Is Empty*

After reading the above section, you may wish to use the CD to follow the guided meditation. In addition, I include instructions below for a meditation that supports the discovery of *Mind is empty*.

Sit in a comfortable posture. Draw your attention inward. Feel stillness in your body, silence in your speech, and spaciousness in your mind. Just feel stillness, silence, and spaciousness while you feel connected and present in your body. Allow time for this.

Bring to awareness an inner challenge or inner vision. As you already have some experience doing, just directly observe that vision. Nakedly look at that vision, dissolving any distance until you are so close to it, it dissipates into a clear, open sky. Allow time for this.

Now look at the mind that observes that dissolution. See who is looking. Who is that mind? Where is that mind? Look directly, nakedly, without judging or analyzing. As you look closer and closer, trying to find the observer, you don't find a solid mind there. There is nothing to be seen. Allow time for this. As you continue to look nakedly, any sense of solid mind or concrete observer dissolves into space and becomes empty. Simply feel this vast, unbounded space. Just be aware and connect with the openness. Mind is that spacious experience. Be conscious and aware of that unbounded space. Rest in the awareness of that unbounded space, without any effort or elaboration. *Mind is empty.*

THE INFORMAL PRACTICE OF *MIND IS EMPTY*

How can we apply the advice *Mind is empty* informally in our everyday life? It is similar to the way we did the formal practice with *Vision is mind*. Here, rather than facing an outer situation or relationship, you are confronting challenges within you. It is your own pain body that becomes the focus. You are challenged by your own inner voices and inner emotions. Sometimes you get angry without understanding why, depressed for no discernible reason; or you experience a sense of loneliness and isolation as you face the challenges of the external world, which constantly bombards you with demands, pressures, and stimulation.

Here is one example of the pain body in everyday life. In the West people who work a weekly nine-to-five job have an interesting relationship to Monday. It produces what I call the Monday-morning face. This is usually in contrast to the Friday-afternoon face. There is a big difference. If you observe people's faces, you can see a more rigid face with perhaps a tinge of sadness or disconnection on Monday morning. By contrast, the face of Friday afternoon is often joyful and playful. So we can bring our awareness in any given moment to this sense of face or identity. Regardless of whether it is Monday or Friday, am I in that sad or disconnected mood? Am I sitting on a rotten karmic cushion? Be conscious of that. The moment I'm conscious of that, I can release that pain body.

In Chapter 1, we spoke of taking the three pills: white, red, and blue. (The white pill is stillness, related to body; the red pill is silence, related to speech; the blue pill is spaciousness, related to mind.) I will repeat the process because I feel it is essential to remember these basic practices. So first you must remember to become aware of yourself. Perhaps your body is rigid and your face tense. This is obvious and easy to become aware of: your body is not relaxed, and you can feel that your expression is the Monday-morning face. You are aware of your pain body. As you connect with stillness, you release tension in your face and body, and as you do so, you are also releasing tension in your ego, which is really the pain body. You feel more relaxed in your body, more relaxed in your breath, and more complete in who you are in this moment. That is the white pill. Remember to do that.

How can we understand and work with pain speech? One student of mine told me he is not worried about his death during the day, but during his sleep he is awakened at three in the morning with thoughts of dying. His mind is actively chattering away, fearfully worried about death. Clearly he needs the medicine of silence. He needs a red pill. First it is important to be aware rather than continuing the internal dialogue, thinking you will find a solution to your dilemma. Don't have another ego conversation. The true medicine here is to hear the silence. Be conscious and open, and bring attention to that voice. Don't struggle with that voice, but host it in the space of awareness. Gradually journey into that voice and experience the silence in and around it. The moment you hear the silence, that voice weakens and dissolves. Slowly you reenter sleep or return to doing your daytime activity. But remember what to do whenever those voices are active: hear the silence. In that way you are taking the red pill.

The third pill is important to take whenever thoughts and emotions such as anger, jealousy, or pride are active. Whenever such thoughts are active, you are creating stories and are less aware of space. Be conscious, and take the blue pill by holding that awareness in and around your thoughts and emotions. The moment you feel spaciousness around and within your thoughts, the thoughts become weak. The thoughts were feeding the ego, and now it also dissolves. When you feel that space open up, you have taken the blue pill of spaciousness.

Take the white, red, or blue pill in relation to whatever challenges you are experiencing. To work with challenges, it is important to make a commitment: "I will remember stillness, silence, and spaciousness five times a day." It won't be effective if you faithfully practice your sitting meditation in the morning but then forget to be conscious during the rest of the day. But committing yourself to remembering inner refuge throughout the day truly protects you. Whenever you need protection, you will find it—through stillness, silence, and spaciousness.

In Conclusion: *Mind Is Empty*

Whatever experience you have created, you observe this nakedly and directly. Observing, you realize that nothing is there; you have the benefit of the first advice of Dawa Gyaltsen if the object of your awareness is no longer solidly there. *Vision is mind.*

What remains is the one who is creating it. When you observe nakedly and do not find anything, it simply takes you to the mind itself. You are able to connect with that mind, that ego, much better. Then the second question applies: What is that mind? Through the same method—naked, open awareness—you observe the mind. Be conscious of the pain body, pain speech, the pain mind. When you are conscious of that, the pain body dissolves, the pain speech dissolves, the pain mind dissolves. What do you find? You find clear, open, and luminous space, which we are calling empty. *Mind is empty.* That is the conclusion of the second line.

In *dzogchen* there is a metaphor: a thief goes to a house to steal and finds the house empty. There is nothing to steal: *Mind is empty.* So when you look at that mind very clearly, nothing is there. If you are disappointed when you look at your mind directly and you do not find anything, ego is still there. When you find nothing and then thoughts and stories rush in because that can't possibly be the right conclusion, that means there is a lack of clear recognition of emptiness. If you simply have clear awareness of that emptiness, it is freeing. Dawa Gyaltsen's advice is to acknowledge and honor what you have discovered: *Mind is empty.*

Finding that emptiness or spaciousness is traditionally expressed by the image of a child who has lost his mother in a crowded marketplace and, after searching, finally finds her. What happens then? You find connection and a deep sense of familiarity. Connecting with the clear and open space of mind is like that. Traditionally, the clear and open space of mind is referred to as the "mother." The mind or awareness that recognizes the mother is referred to as the "son," or the child. In the natural mind they are inseparable, and when you recognize their union, the result is dynamic energy, which is experienced as the free and spontaneous expression of virtuous qualities. Experiencing this is like feeling impoverished and then suddenly discovering that you have been wealthy all along. Your ego, your pain body, speech, and mind, your sense of separateness and not belonging—all this becomes the door through which you pass to encounter the sacred, the divine, your true self, the recognition of being complete as you are in this moment. Knowing this, when you encounter *Mind is empty*, remain in that recognition. Meditation is staying with awareness of that emptiness. That is the realization and the encouragement of the second line, *Mind is empty*.

CHAPTER SIX

EMPTINESS IS CLEAR LIGHT

Mind is empty has taught us that we cannot find a solid inherent mind; when we look inward with naked awareness, we find spaciousness, openness, emptiness. Many people equate *emptiness* with nothingness. It is not uncommon for a person to feel a sense of loss or fear when encountering emptiness. For some, the pain body is their identity and, in a strange way, their support. Through pain people find friends, and they may feel supported by others who suffer in similar ways. So when the discovery is made that your identity is not solidly there and a completely new space opens up, this space can be pervaded by a sense of loss, and emptiness appears as lack. The experience of fear may accompany this loss. To conclude that the mind is empty in this way is incorrect. This is the error of nihilism, a pessimistic assumption that space is empty and therefore is nothing.

The empty mind is not "nothing." Emptiness is everything. Emptiness is fullness. Emptiness is completeness. The term *dzogchen* itself means "great completeness." In this emptiness, in this space, everything is spontaneously perfected. Joy is here, love is here. Compassion and forgiveness are here. Confidence is here. Every quality that you can name is fully present in spaciousness. It is a matter of being aware long enough to nourish and ripen the experience of openness. It is a matter of familiarity.

So Dawa Gyaltsen's third advice, *Emptiness is clear light,* is encouragement on the path. It means emptiness is not just empty and nothing; it is clear light, the source of every quality. His advice is protection from falling into nihilist denial and depression, and encourages the meditator to allow the time to be aware and connect with the infinite possibilities that are available.

We have been working with the "famous person," the vision or object, which we have discovered is not there externally as we previously experienced. Then we continued our investigation to discover that there is no solidity in the subject, the observer, either. As a result of this, we experience a sense of clear open space. Now we continue in meditation to explore the relationship with the clear space of being, sitting comfortably and drawing our attention inward. I am looking with the same naked awareness, open and conscious of the emptiness. I am fully aware of that spaciousness, that emptiness. If you comment to yourself, "Oh, I understand," that is a movement of thought, and that thought does not understand this space fully. Without following any thoughts, simply be aware of emptiness, of spaciousness. Awareness itself is clear light.

When clear light manifests outwardly, it is possible to perceive lights and visions, and people do have clear-light experiences in dreams, in sleep, and in deep meditation. In near-death, or, according to the teachings, in after-death experiences, people also encounter these lights, which are related with inner awareness. However it manifests, when we speak of clear light, its real meaning is pure awareness—the luminosity, vitality, and warmth of the awareness of spaciousness.

It is important to be fully aware of the space that was previously occupied by our vision and our pain identity. That is the important point here. In psychotherapy it sometimes seems that the goal is to understand and resolve conflict and pain by reflecting, analyzing, and thinking, which is a difficult enough task. And when a person is able to overcome pain by these means, it is possible to conclude: "Okay, now I'm clear; I understand my personal conflict deeply, and now I am no longer troubled by this problem. I can move on. I am ready for the next challenge." According to the teachings, that attitude is mistaken in that it doesn't go far enough. What is lacking in psychological methods is the cultivation of the *absence of problem*. In most forms of psychotherapy, we fail to become aware of the space that the problem had occupied or obscured, and we are not taught to cultivate it through further attention. Awareness of the space is not acknowledged as important, and therefore we do not become familiar with it.

In the process of healing, when someone is able to resolve the pain body, speech, or mind, that is only half the journey. Only half of the work is done. To truly mature as a human being, the second half of the work of healing needs to happen. According to these teachings, the maturing of the second half occurs as you cultivate or maintain awareness of space. That is why it is important to understand *Emptiness is clear light* in the correct philosophical sense, so as not to fall into an extreme position, the nihilist idea that this means "nothingness" in a negative sense. And it is also important to understand *Emptiness is clear light* experientially, by following the path of liberation from pain. Even if our suffering seems to have ceased, we do not stop our work of healing, but instead we go on being continuously aware of awareness itself. This light of awareness is what recognizes emptiness or spaciousness. That is why *Emptiness is clear light* is the third line of advice.

Clear light is innate awareness, self-awareness. When working with a particular situation and observing it directly and nakedly, we discover that the famous person or situation is not outside, but is a creation of mind. *Vision is mind.* Then we observe mind and discover that this famous person is not inside either. *Mind is empty.* When we are unfamiliar with what is not there, we conclude that it is nothing. But emptiness is full. Being aware of the fullness of spaciousness is the experience of *Emptiness is clear light.* Being aware of that emptiness, tasting that emptiness, feeling connected to that emptiness, *being* that emptiness, is what is referred to as clear light. It is important to emphasize this because otherwise it is so easy for people to lose connection to awareness.

As we have explored, when our pain body, pain speech, and pain mind are active, we perceive all sorts of problems and struggles "out there," because our mind—the inner famous person who is engaging the problems—is outwardly active, and this outward focus continues to feed the unexamined ego. Through these practices, the outer famous person or situation dissolves, and then the focus shifts and the inner storyteller dissolves, until there is nothing to engage. You remain with nothing, but it is not "nothing" in the depressing sense—it is full openness. It's very important to become familiar with and aware of that openness after you dissolve the famous outer and inner person.

The image of sky, clouds, and sun illustrates the healing process we have been exploring. Inside us we have spaciousness, the sky. Our thoughts or emotions are like clouds, and whether they are gentle puffs or thunderheads, they obscure the sky. The sun stands for the light and warmth of awareness. So through this practice of awareness, we clear away the clouds of thoughts, emotions, sensations, and recollections—everything that makes up the inner and outer famous person. Again, we are clearing the clouds through the method of nakedly observing. We nakedly observe thoughts, feelings, sensations, and recollections, and we nakedly observe the one who is observing. What remains is the clear sky. In that unobstructed clarity of the inner sky, it is natural for sunlight to pervade space. So sunshine is that clear light of awareness. It is visible because the clouds are removed: both thoughts and the thinker dissolve.

Many people are either very engaged with their inner clouds or worried that the clouds will come again. They are caught up in how to handle the clouds when they appear; and yet, when the clouds go, they miss them! So they are never able to fully appreciate the clear sky. One time I was in a group teaching a beautiful Bön practice called sky gazing, in which we gaze at the actual sky as a support for connecting with the open expanse of our natural minds. One person raised his hand and said, "I'm looking at the sky, but what am I supposed to see? I don't see anything." We were looking at this incredibly open blue sky, and he was saying, "I'm not seeing anything." He was only familiar with stuff, not with clarity itself. So he needed to become conscious that he *was* seeing it. Seeing the open expanse, the awareness of openness, is light. Similarly, when we look inward and don't find anything, we may conclude that there is nothing. That is a very fundamental error. It is important to be conscious of that openness as a presence, not an absence. Awareness of that openness can be experienced like a taste. Sometimes, it is referred to as having "the taste of emptiness."

Another example that I give of the pervasive power of the awareness of openness is the experience of winning the lottery. Here is a positive example that many of us have fantasized about at least once: You win the hundred million dollar lottery. Imagine that! Somebody is always winning it, so why not you? So when you win the lottery, you clearly experience some joy. And let's say in the midst of this joy, your dear old Toyota breaks down. You are driving along the highway when suddenly it stalls. You hear a grinding sound, manage to pull over to the side of the road, and stop the car. You are sad that your old car is dying, but deep inside there is also a happy feeling as you realize that you are completely ready for a nice new car. This is the right time! The joy of winning the lottery is present through the sadness of losing your car. After winning the lottery, you work and eat and sleep with that joy of winning pervading all those experiences, so even the loss of your car is pervaded by joy. A similar thing happens when you experience the vast awareness of spaciousness. That taste of emptiness begins to pervade all of your experiences, both good and bad.

Clarity is not only being aware of that space but also the experiences arising from that space. For instance, joy can spontaneously arise. Even in that joy, awareness is still there. So having that awareness is very important. The teachings guide us to be aware of that space, conscious of that space. Aware, conscious, connected, we are hosting that space. That is what we are referring to with *Emptiness is clear light.*

GUIDED MEDITATION PRACTICE OF *EMPTINESS IS CLEAR LIGHT*

After reading the above section, you may wish to use the CD to follow the guided meditation. Additionally, I include instructions for a meditation below to support the discovery of *Emptiness is clear light.*

Sit in a comfortable posture. Draw your attention inward. Feel stillness in your body, silence in your speech, and spaciousness in your mind. Just feel stillness, silence, and spaciousness while you feel connected and present in your body. Allow time for this.

Once again, bring to awareness whatever vision you have been working with, or your experience of this present moment. *Vision is mind.* Just look directly, nakedly, closer and closer, until the clouds of your vision dissipate revealing an open sky. Experience a sense of expansiveness and openness. Recognize and be aware of that openness. Allow time for this.

Now look at who is looking, who is observing. Look inward; look closer; look nakedly, clearly without any analysis, look closer, closer, closer until the observer dissolves, disappears. This inner cloud, this observer, dissolves in the inner space. *Mind is empty.* Allow time to experience this.

As the observer dissolves, be aware and remain connected with that boundless inner space. Feel that boundless space like a vast desert sky, so vast there are no boundaries. *Emptiness is clear light.*

As you experience continuously that vast, boundless, infinite space, there is a chance of gradually losing your awareness of that space, so be aware of that, and refresh that sense of awareness of openness. It is not just "empty"; it is clear light. There is luminous awareness in that vast space, and that awareness is lively and vivid and fresh. Be aware of that awareness as you experience vast, boundless space.

Being *aware of the awareness* of that boundless space is the focus of this third session of the meditation practice. Continuously rest in that boundless space. Continuously be aware of your awareness of that boundless space, rather than getting lost or falling into that vast space. That is the importance of this third session of the practice. Rest in the awareness of that unbounded space without any effort or elaboration. *Emptiness is clear light.*

The Informal Practice of *Emptiness Is Clear Light*

What is the informal practice of *Emptiness is clear light?* First, remember the accomplishments of the previous two lines: *Vision is mind* and *Mind is empty*. Every time you face an external challenge, bring to mind *Vision is mind*. Immediately you will realize you are facing an internal challenge, and as you are conscious and aware of that, feel the spaciousness that becomes available. Once you feel this openness, trust it, and continue to be present and aware of it. Remember and recognize the importance of being aware of that spaciousness. You may experience this common tendency, "Okay, I feel a little open with my boss, now I can go do my stuff." Don't stop at this point. Continue experiencing the spaciousness until that inner recognition leads to a sense of warmth and gratitude, because you have reconnected with the space of being and are connected with the nourishment that becomes available. Knowing that it is important to be *aware* of the openness is the key. Remain present and experience the warmth that emerges as the result.

The path to knowing oneself as described by Dawa Gyaltsen and other *dzogchen* masters is not to avoid experiences. In some spiritual traditions, certain experiences are avoided or renounced. We avoid what poisons us. Here we are not being encouraged to renounce experience, but rather to bring naked and direct awareness to the experience. In that way any experience becomes a door. Strong emotion is a door. You cannot stop or control emotion. You can suppress it, but this does not lead to a good result, for nothing that is suppressed goes away. Here we are guided to look directly. Basically greet, shake hands, and say hello to what arises in your experience. When you look at it nakedly, no matter how strong the emotion, awareness is more powerful. No matter how strong the negative affliction, when we engage directly, whatever arises in experience is weaker than awareness itself.

Awareness is not a belief, slogan, or affirmation. It is hard for us to believe that fear, or anger, or jealousy can be overcome by observing it. *Don't I need a stronger weapon or a more sophisticated technique?* you may be thinking. It is hard to understand that naked awareness itself is even possible when emotion is so strong, let alone understand that the emotion could dissolve by observing it. It seems impossible until you do it. Do it with naked awareness, not with the doubting mind, which is saying, "This is impossible." Very likely, if you are saying it is impossible you are observing your anger with a fearful or doubting mind. So the observer is very important. The observer has got to be naked. If you observe nakedly, it happens. When it happens, you trust it is possible again. When you trust, the more likely it is that you will apply this each time challenges arise in your life. This is the beginning of true integration in everyday life. You do it because you know it helps, and you know it helps because you have witnessed the dissolution of your pain body, pain speech, and pain mind as you experienced them directly and nakedly. So when a moment of challenge happens, when you remember to enter the inner refuge through one of the three doorways of stillness, silence, and spaciousness, it is important to give yourself credit.

Whether you are walking in a beautiful park or a crowded shopping mall, walk in the awareness of openness. If you are in a line at the post office, stand hosting that awareness of unbounded space. Riding on a bus, sit in open awareness. The moment before you go to sleep, bring open awareness to your heart and rest there. Remaining in open awareness will affect your next conversation, the flow of your day, your dreams, and your sleep. That awareness is powerful medicine. Remembering open awareness throughout the activities of day and night, your life will flourish.

In Conclusion: *Emptiness Is Clear Light*

Each of these lines is connected to the other. When we realize the first line, it is naturally connected to the second one, and so on. It is important to recognize these connections happening in your own experience. So it can be beneficial to work on the same issue or challenge for a period of time, bringing to mind the same famous person or situation each time you sit down to meditate. Do this until you can see a shift, and notice the development through these stages. Suppose I am feeling fearful deep inside, and therefore I am manifesting anger and projecting it out on someone and seeing a famous person outside. Through the power of practicing with the first line of advice, *Vision is mind*, I no longer experience this power to disturb me as coming from outside. Then, with naked awareness I see that famous person—me, my own mind—is not solid, as I realize *Mind is empty*. All dissolves into *Emptiness is clear light.* In this openness, everything is here, the source of all knowledge and qualities are in this openness. Here I rest my attention, and at any opportunity, I am aware of that space as a space that nourishes my inner being. Like sunshine to a flower, that awareness nourishes me. That "me" is not the pain me, but the openness me, the bliss me. Because I am more familiar with pain identity, pain speech, and the pain mind, when I feel openness I must remind myself to recognize it. Awareness is powerful, but my recognition of it and my connection to it is weak, so it is important that I cultivate strength and familiarity with the awareness of openness at this point. That is what we are doing in the third session of practice, *Emptiness is clear light.*

ABIDE, DISSOLVE, CONTINUE: INSTRUCTION FOR MAINTAINING AWARENESS

Many find it hard to maintain what they have achieved in meditation. If you achieve some space, it is hard to maintain. If you connect with silence, it is hard to maintain. How is it maintained? The meditation instruction is "Abide, dissolve, continue." To *abide* means to enter through the doorways of stillness, silence, and spaciousness and to rest in open awareness. *Dissolve* means that as the pain body manifests, nakedly observe it; directly observe the pain voice if that is what disturbs you; observe the pain mind, if that is disturbing you. As you observe nakedly and directly, whatever you observe dissolves.

There are three analogies used for the degree of effort in your practice connected with "dissolving." When your meditation practice is well established, it is possible to experience the pain body, speech, and mind dissolving like snow falling into the ocean. The sense of abiding is so deep and vast that as things arise in the mind, they simply dissolve the way a snowflake would in the ocean. When your practice of abiding is less established, it is necessary to use some effort because the habit of identifying with the pain body, speech, and mind is still present. This effort is analogous to sun hitting frost on a windowpane. The frost, or apparent solidity of our pain, melts in the sunlight of our naked awareness. The third analogy refers to what we all may experience when we first establish a meditation practice, and describes the most effortful relationship to our pain body, speech, and mind, because our tendency to experience what arises in the mind as "me" or "who I am" is strong, and we are easily carried away with thinking and elaborating. This effort involves being mindful that, in fact, you are experiencing pain. There is strength and precision involved in bringing one's attention directly to the stillness, silence, or spaciousness, the moment you become aware of pain. It is similar to hitting a nail on the head or threading a needle, in the degree of effort used in focusing.

When what you observe dissolves, continue in the same state—aware of the awareness of spaciousness. Most of us need to practice abiding and dissolving many times before getting a sense of continuing. Once you become more familiar with the experience of dissolving, you continue. Gradually, as you master the practice, dissolving happens effortlessly. Eventually, you simply rest in open awareness. You will need to dissolve less and less, because you are more stable in open awareness. Over time, your practice will mature and become effortless.

CHAPTER SEVEN

CLEAR LIGHT IS UNION

There are two words in Dawa Gyaltsen's advice that we need to examine more closely: *clear* and *light*. *Clear* refers to spaciousness, openness. *Light* refers to awareness, or being aware of that openness. In the example of the sky, clouds, and sun, *clear* refers to the sky, and *light* refers to the sunlight. The word *clear* implies clearing. In this case, experientially, with the work of nakedly observing the external and internal famous person, you clear the pain body, pain speech, and the pain mind, so we are experiencing openness at this point. So *clear* refers to that openness (your perception of which was previously obscured by the pain body, pain speech, and the pain mind), and *light* refers to the awareness of that openness.

Experientially, when the grasping mind and its object dissolve, you perceive "no thing" and may conclude that nothing exists—the error of nihilism. The antidote is to experience *Emptiness is clear light*. But there is another extreme you can fall into—the extreme of eternalism. As we have been working with the first three lines, we have been experiencing the dissolution of the pain body, pain speech, and the pain mind. Finding the inner clear space and recognizing the awareness of that space is like sunshine pervading a clear, open sky. Once you experience that, there can be a sense of attachment to the experience: "Oh, this is a great feeling! This is great spaciousness. This is great bliss. I want this to last forever. I want to give this to others. This will be my gift to others!" Meanwhile, you have lost the experience by grasping it. In so doing, you lose the connection to the base, ground, space, mother, essence. The moment you lose it, what you began to feel as bliss and light begins to turn to pain again. You have a short glimpse, you grasp it, and then you lose it. "Oh, I had such a beautiful and comfortable and blissful experience." How long did it last? Usually it is very short. Why is it so short? Simply because you have grasped and not understood the inseparable state of openness and awareness. Falling into the trap of eternalism, your grasping arises. Falling into nihilism, you experience a sense of nothing. So in this fourth session, it is important not to fall into either extreme. Here, the advice of Dawa Gyaltsen is *Clear light is union*.

Clear and light—union. Sky and sunshine—union. Space and awareness—union. Openness and awareness—union. Emptiness and clarity—union. The sky and sunshine are not separate; space and light are not separate; openness and awareness are not separate. It is important to experience it without separating it, and so you rest in that inseparable state of emptiness and clarity. Philosophically, the important point here is that there is no separation between space and awareness, subject and object, matter and mind. So you abide in the inseparable state of openness and awareness. That is the key here: *Clear light is union*.

What does this mean on a personal level? Perhaps you have been working with a specific issue or appearance or object as you have been following along with the meditations in this book and on the CD. With *Vision is mind*, you discovered that the specific object or appearance dissolved as you brought naked awareness to your experience. With *Mind is empty*, the subject dissolved.

With *Emptiness is clear light,* the emphasis is on awareness of that spaciousness, and now with *Clear light is union,* the guidance is to experience the inseparability of awareness and openness.

Let's go through this again as a meditation practice: When you close your eyes and observe your vision, you find that there is nothing solid there, so the vision dissolves. The mind is the one creating it; therefore, *Vision is mind.* Next you explore: What is the mind? Looking for that mind with naked awareness, you cannot find any inherent solid existence of that mind. So mind, the subject, dissolves and you feel the presence of inner spaciousness. *Mind is empty.* Resting in that space, you are aware of that space. When clouds clear, the sun naturally shines. You see sunlight pervading the spaciousness with *Emptiness is clear light.* Now we become aware that there is no separation possible with the sky and sunlight. In the space before you, can you say this is where the space is and this is the light? No, you cannot separate the space from the light. Internally, when you experience openness and the awareness of that openness, you cannot say, "Oh, this is the awareness and this is the openness." They are nondual. But in meditation, to discover this, you have to be aware of it. Whether or not you know this doesn't affect the nature of mind itself. But for you, knowing this, you liberate suffering, and not knowing this, you get caught up in delusion. So in this practice of *Clear light is union,* simply be aware of that nondual, inseparable state.

When people go on vacation and lie down on a beautiful beach under a clear, sun-drenched sky, they may feel quite relaxed. Is it a good meditation? Well, you might say it is a kind of meditation, but it is clearly not what we are talking about here. There is a lack of being conscious of that spaciousness. The state of mind while lying on the beach is perhaps closer to that of a cat seated in a sunny shop window. It looks as if the cat is meditating. It is still; it appears spacious, but it is not being particularly aware of that. Awareness is the important part. *Clear light is union*, being aware of that union, that inseparable state, is key.

GUIDED MEDITATION PRACTICE OF *CLEAR LIGHT IS UNION*

After reading the above section, you may wish to use the CD to follow the guided meditation. Additionally, I include the following instructions for a meditation that supports the discovery of *Clear light is union*.

Sit in a comfortable posture. Draw your attention inward. Feel stillness in your body, silence in your speech, and spaciousness in your mind. Just feel stillness, silence, and spaciousness, while you feel connected and present in your body. Allow time for this.

Now, once again, bring to conscious awareness that vision, that object of ego that you have been working with. Bring it to conscious awareness, and through naked and direct observation, look closer and closer until it disappears and you sense a clear sky. Rest for a moment in that clear sky. *Vision is mind.*

With the second practice, *Mind is empty*, look inward at who is observing that vision, that object. Look at that mind with direct, naked awareness, without further elaboration or thinking; look closer and closer until you don't find that mind. It dissolves, becoming spacious, empty, a "nothing" that is clear and open. You experience vast, unbounded space. Just rest there for a moment. *Mind is empty.*

Avoid falling into the experience of vastness by being aware of the awareness of vastness. Just feel vast awareness, the luminosity of mind. *Emptiness is clear light.* It is clear. It is vivid. It is alert. It is vital. Be aware of the awareness of the unbounded space.

Even as you are experiencing this luminosity, this awareness, this alertness, just feel its connection with the vastness, with the experience of unbounded spaciousness. Even as your experience is energetic and vibrant and luminous, still it is connected with the vast space, the ground, the base, the mother, the inner essence. It is connected with that inner essence. There is no separation; there is union. That is why we say, *Clear light is union.*

Be aware that there is no separation. Be aware of nonduality: there is no separation between openness and awareness, no separation between clarity and emptiness. Just realize, experience, and know the nondual state. Experience awareness while experiencing emptiness. Experience emptiness while experiencing awareness. Without effort, rest in nondual awareness.

THE INFORMAL PRACTICE OF *CLEAR LIGHT IS UNION*

You have been applying the practice informally to your everyday experiences, so let's reflect back on what that has meant. We have talked about holding the space of stillness, silence, and spaciousness throughout the day in relation to yourself, your family and close relationships, and at work, or when involved in the larger community. In these three places—self, close relationships, and the larger world—you have been encouraged to take the three pills of stillness, silence, and space. Perhaps you have been successful with that. What might that success look like?

Let's continue with the example of you and your boss. You go to work and try to be present with the discomfort of the situation with your boss. You hold stillness and feel protected. You hold that spaciousness and feel good. Now at some point you are able to engage with your boss from that open place. You feel quite good talking and engaging. "Wow, this is amazing. Now I feel quite good with my boss." You lose the motivation to continue to connect with spaciousness, because you are feeling okay. As a result of the practice you feel spacious and open and clear and comfortable, but that experience becomes just another object of ego if you lose the connection to the base, the mother, the space. Clear light is not union for you anymore. You had it, then you lost it. You lost it because you were grasping it. *Clear light is union* is the antidote to what we don't have when we lose it.

So be aware of the space as you engage in the activity of life. Maintain the connection between the space and the action, the experiencer and the experiences, the base and the appearances, emptiness and clarity. To maintain that experience is very important. Simply put: when you are dealing with things, continue to be aware of space. When you are aware of spaciousness and can deal with a situation and not get caught up or lost in the activity, but can continuously refresh and maintain awareness of the space, that is *Clear light is union* in everyday life.

In Conclusion: Clear Light Is Union

We get so caught up in objects or the imagination that ego created, and yet, when we realize our state of being caught up, it dissolves. Remember at this point to see who is looking—that also dissolves. That becomes empty. Is everything empty? No, it is clear light. We realize the experience of awareness. We can get caught up in the vividness of our experience, and so we say

Clear light is union. There is no separation between the emptiness of experience and the vividness of experience. Each realization leads you to the next, which illuminates places where you might go off course, and then, guides your practice back into connection.

CHAPTER EIGHT

UNION IS GREAT BLISS

Union refers to openness and the awareness of openness. As mentioned before, openness is the mother and awareness is the son or child. Openness, the mother, is emptiness. Clarity, the child, is awareness. Openness is sky; awareness is sunlight. Sky and sunlight are not separate. Openness is not separate from awareness of that openness. It is not that union itself is bliss, but from that union, from that recognition of openness, bliss arises.

The notion of pain body, pain speech, and the pain mind—the whole existence of your personality and characteristics—is caused by not knowing your true self. The definition of not knowing yourself is ignorance, which is the root cause of suffering. But from the union of space and the knowing of space, another experience of yourself arises. That union gives birth to a new sense of self, a new sense of being. That new sense of yourself has a deep quality of bliss—the bliss of infinite qualities. That is what *Union is great bliss* means. Bliss is just one experience. All qualities, such as love, compassion, joy, and equanimity, will naturally manifest from that union, from experiencing the natural mind. If union is experienced, all these qualities will naturally manifest. What kind of experiences would you love to manifest in your life? If you ask the ego, it will make a long list. Ego thinks it needs so much to secure itself. But in this union, what you truly need at any given time or place in your life will spontaneously manifest.

Although the positive, healing qualities will spontaneously become available as we recognize and trust openness, often as we practice meditation we may experience layers to the pain identity. For instance, you may bring your attention to an experience of anxiety or discomfort. As you do so, you become aware of the presence of anger. If you remain in awareness and host the anger, it releases. As it does, you may become aware of an underlying fear. And if you bring naked awareness to the fear and host the fear, as it releases, you can taste an underlying sadness. As you continue to bring awareness to that sadness and host it, it dissolves. As sadness is released, you come to a much deeper stillness, silence, and spaciousness. Once you are in that space and aware of that space, there is a quality of warmth available. You discover it because it is no longer obscured by the pain identity. That is the warmth of that union, which Dawa Gyaltsen refers to as bliss. In that bliss of union, joy naturally arises. Not only can joy arise from that union, but confidence comes from that union—blissful confidence—because the pain body of anger and fear and sadness has dissolved, and the resulting openness that becomes available gives birth to the bliss of confidence. Whenever a painful experience dissolves, a positive quality emerges, as long as you remain in that union long enough. That is how we discover *Union is great bliss.*

So you begin with the famous person who is the apparent source of your pain, and by the end of this practice, the object of pain becomes the discovery of bliss. Your pain becomes bliss. You start with pain and you end with bliss. Of course, you have followed clear and specific steps to become conscious of your pain and bring naked awareness to it, and as a result, the changeable painful body becomes the changeless body of bliss.

The experience of great bliss is born from that union of space and light, openness and awareness. Union is there, bliss is there. The only reason we don't experience this in our everyday life is that space is occupied with pain body, pain speech, and the pain mind. Thus, we don't feel the connection, and we are not aware of that union. But as we work in meditation with the five lines of Dawa Gyaltsen's heart instructions, we come to a deep and clear space in ourselves. At least for a moment we are opening up with the pain body, pain speech, and the pain mind. You are open and you are aware that sky and sun are unified. You feel a sense of awareness of that inseparable state, and you feel a deep sense of bliss and a deep sense of joy. Deep peace is experienced there.

Simply be aware of that warmth, that bliss. You are having this experience because you are in that union, that inseparable state. When that becomes available in your practice, feel it fully. As you bring attention to your heart, and connect with the spaciousness, you can feel the expansion of that bliss throughout your body. It is possible to feel this not by forcing anything, but by simply being aware. As awareness travels, bliss travels. So it is important to feel that expansion through your entire body, and also in the face, where we often hold the expression of our sadness. Once you connect with that sense of union in meditation, you will experience a feeling of warmth. As you bring awareness to your heart, you can feel the expansion of that warmth through your entire body. Awareness, like sunlight, expands, and light will naturally expand beyond the bounds of your body. In this way you effortlessly radiate love, or joy, or whatever quality you are experiencing. Experience the bliss of positive qualities, and invite an experience of the pain body. Bring that sense of joy to the way you identify yourself, and to the ways you experience sickness. Bring bliss there. Become aware of the way in which you talk to people when you are rushed or tense, and feel the bliss radiating through those constrictions. As you become aware, you will hear your voice changing from harsh to gentle. Your inner pain voice will shift its qualities because of bliss. In the same way, the experience of bliss can pervade the habitual negative and depressive patterns of mind you experience. Instead of being vigilant, scanning for problems, or engaged in worried problem solving, you will have more positive, productive, and kinder thoughts that are naturally solution-oriented. In this way, your experiences of your body, your voice, and your mind will transform. Become aware of these transformations. This will encourage and support you to continuously engage your practice.

Guided Meditation Practice of *Union Is Great Bliss*

After reading the above section, you may wish to use the CD to follow the guided meditation. Practice this until you feel a shift and begin to taste the experience of *Union is great bliss*. Additionally, I include instructions below for a meditation that supports the discovery of *Union is great bliss*.

Sit in a comfortable posture. Draw your attention inward. Feel stillness in your body, silence in your speech, and spaciousness in your mind. Just feel stillness, silence, and spaciousness while you feel connected and present in your body. Allow time for this.

Whatever vision you are working on, continue with the same vision and bring it to conscious awareness. Observe that vision nakedly without thought, judgment, or analysis. Observe directly, going closer and closer until it dissipates into an experience that is open like the sky. Be aware and feel a sense of clear sky. *Vision is mind.*

Now look: Who is observing that vision? Who is looking? Look inward; look closer and closer. Look directly, nakedly, until the mind that is looking dissolves. You don't find that mind; all you find is emptiness, vast space. Rest in that vast space without any effort. *Mind is empty.*

Without falling into or getting lost in vastness, be aware of the awareness of vastness. That is *Emptiness is clear light.* That vastness is luminous because awareness is there. Be aware of that awareness. *Emptiness is clear light.* Be aware of the alertness, vividness, vitality, luminosity of this moment.

Without grasping at that vitality, that light, that energy, be aware of its connection to that vastness, that space, that emptiness. That is what we mean by *Clear light is union.* They are inseparable. Abide in that nondual state, that inseparable state of openness and awareness, emptiness and clarity. Rest there without any effort.

This last session is *Union is great bliss.* Continuously rest in that union, that openness and awareness, feeling completely boundless, feeling this vast, infinite space around and within you, feeling that deep sense of stillness throughout all appearance and forms, feeling a deep sense of silence throughout this awareness, while being fully aware, alert, vivid, and energetic. Resting continuously in that nondual state, gradually experience a sense of warmth, a sense of joy in your heart. Just feel it. Allow it. It is there. That very natural and deep sense of joy is the joy of being, the joy of who you are, and the joy of knowing yourself. That is why we call it *Union is great bliss.* Allow it; you will feel it. As you feel it, allow it to expand through your heart and through the rest of your body, through your flesh, bones, blood, skin, through your face, your eyes—through every cell of your body.

Wherever you may detect the presence of depression or sadness, this inner bliss transforms and blesses those places. Allow the warmth and joy to pervade throughout your body and mind. You don't have to do anything. Just be aware and feel the natural movement of warmth throughout your body, emotions, and mind.

Allow bliss, like pure medicine, to move through your body wherever you have pain or sickness, or wherever you are concerned about getting sick. Allow the warmth to move and clear those inner obstacles. This inner bliss is medicine. You don't need to make any effort; just allow it and feel it. It is happening in you spontaneously.

THE INFORMAL PRACTICE OF *UNION IS GREAT BLISS*

In doing the informal practice of *Union is great bliss*, it is important to understand that the five steps of Dawa Gyaltsen's teaching are connected to each other. Therefore, throughout the day, as you hold and maintain a connection with stillness, silence, and spaciousness within you, many opportunities to experience bliss will arise—if you are sensitive enough and able to experience a subtle awareness of it.

As the pain body, pain voice, and the pain mind dissolve, what remains? Draw your attention inside and look: Joy is there. Bliss is there. If, when you close your eyes, there are many disturbing emotions and thoughts, then bliss is not there. You experience pain outside and pain inside. But as you become more familiar with the practice, when you go within and bring awareness to that space, the warmth of connection will be there. In stillness, when you draw attention within, warmth is there. Be open to feeling that warmth. As inner clouds dissipate, inner sunshine is there.

Feel that warmth throughout your day, particularly when you are not moving, talking, or thinking too much. Take advantage of those ordinary moments. While riding a bus, waiting to board a plane, or standing in line at the post office, draw your attention inward and try to connect with and feel the inner warmth of awareness through stillness, silence, and spaciousness. Become as familiar with it as you can, as often as you can, throughout the day. Refresh your commitment to yourself as I have suggested, with the metaphor of taking three pills. And every evening before you go to sleep, review the day and see whether you remembered to do this.

Once you have recognized, connected with, and felt that warmth, try to express it. Perhaps you are talking with someone when you notice that you feel slightly annoyed by the person. At the moment it is not terrible, but it could get worse. As soon as you become aware of that feeling of annoyance, draw your attention within and feel the stillness, hear the silence, or recognize the spaciousness. Connect with the warmth that becomes available, and let that warmth be reflected in your voice. Not only will the words that come from that inner source be kinder or more creative, but you will be able to see this reflected in the other person as warmth comes back toward you.

Again and again, remember to bring awareness to the inner refuge and connect with the awareness of openness directly—the place of union—until it pervades all of your experiences. Actively intend to do this five times daily, particularly when you are challenged or irritated in any way. Particularly at those times, connect with the place of union and express warmth in your speech or actions, or simply host warm thoughts and feelings. Making a commitment in this way and refreshing that commitment daily are very helpful, and will support your progress on the path.

IN CONCLUSION: *UNION IS GREAT BLISS*

The conclusion here is the same as for the first four lines of advice, because every part of the practice is connected with the others. You will not have experiences of bliss unless you recognize *Vision is mind* and follow the sequence step by step. Whatever relationship or situation you are working on, try to continue from *Vision is mind* through *Union is great bliss* until you turn that painful thought, action, or state of being into warmth.

If you have not yet experienced the transformation from pain into bliss, do not change the focus of your practice to something different. It is important to have one clear experience of pain becoming bliss. In the end, this practice is about the relationship you have to your experience. You can bring additional topics to your meditation practice, but continue to host the topic you originally chose, so that you can experience that pain releasing into bliss. That is the goal of the practice. Once you experience bliss, it is important not to grasp at the bliss; simply appreciate the shift. You will be able to shift all your experiences of suffering and pain, as long as you look directly at your experience with naked awareness, host your experience with warmth, and trust open awareness.

CHAPTER NINE

THE TREASURY OF THE NATURAL MIND

So, now you have been introduced to the treasury of your own natural mind through discovering and resting in the inner refuge, and through meditation on the five lines of Dawa Gyaltsen. How can you live closer to this treasury? Throughout the day, again and again turn toward the inner refuge. Each time you glimpse the openness of being, you discover the gifs of openness, awareness, and warmth. This refuge is your support. Each time you turn toward the inner refuge, you are reconnected to the sacred in life. Instead of being restlessly driven by the imagined poverty of ego, you discover that your natural being is most precious and valuable. When you are aware of the unbounded spaciousness of being, everything lines up and is interconnected. When you experience that interconnectedness, every single breath you take is a healing breath. Every inhalation heals and nourishes. Every exhalation naturally releases the accumulation of effortful striving, like a river flowing into a vast ocean. Every single exhalation of your breath is a purification of great awareness.

As you abide in open awareness, this union of openness and awareness births immeasurable love, compassion, joy, and equanimity. The birthing of these qualities is referred to as dynamic energy. It is possible to feel a sense of joy in your heart at this moment. You are resting in your body, resting in your breath, connecting with the spaciousness of your mind: everything is supporting you. If you simply allow it, love is here. If you simply allow it, compassion is here. If you simply allow yourself to feel equanimity, it is here. As you are open, you are clear; therefore you allow, and you are able to see, what exists in you. All these enlightened qualities are primordially perfected in being. When there is no obscuration, you can experience this. Each time you are aware of a specific quality, you are nourished. When you rest in that inseparable state of openness and awareness, the inseparable state of mother and child, you are nourished.

The *dzogchen* teachings tell us that abiding in the nature of mind is sufficient for spiritual enlightenment. For that reason, there is not as much emphasis on cultivating compassion as in other traditions; the idea is that as we rest in the nature of mind, compassion will arise naturally. For those who are able to devote a significant amount of time to the practice of abiding in awareness, this teaching makes sense. But what about those of us who lead busy lives and don't have hours to devote to sitting in meditation? For most ordinary people, for whom thoughts and emotions are so much a part of our everyday life, it is important to be more aware of the situations in which we find ourselves. For example, if you look at your life to identify what drains you, you might find quite a number of things that are making you age faster, behaviors that may lead to sickness, or habit patterns that may interfere with your relationships. The more those stressful patterns are present in you, the more you become self-critical and are filled with judgment.

Perhaps you are not aware of why you feel so drained of energy. When I first got a "smartphone," I couldn't understand why the battery lasted such a short time. Then someone advised me that there were ways to save battery life, and in particular that there were many unnecessary applications running on my phone that I wasn't aware of; these unnecessary apps were draining the life of the battery. If I simply identified them and shut them down, my battery lasted longer. In a similar way, there are some patterns of which you are completely unaware and it seems you never get a break from them. It might be a pervasive anxiety that accompanies you throughout your day. An application is running, but you are unaware of it. At the end of your day you are drained and exhausted. Of course, if you simply abide in the nature of mind, those patterns of hope and fear will not be there while you are meditating. But that means you will have to abide for a long enough time for the patterns to clear. When you stop meditating and continue with your life, the patterns may return. So it is necessary to bring more awareness and look more deeply into the details of your personal patterns while you are in the process of living your life.

Most people would agree that they don't want to be drained by life—they would like to find life nourishing. In meditation, when you connect with unbounded space, the mother, the source of being, this is like unplugging from whatever drains you. But even when you are not meditating, you can also unplug at any moment when you connect with the unbounded space through bringing your awareness to stillness, silence, and spaciousness. And then you are free. As long as you can stay connected, you are free of draining patterns. So first, unplug from whatever drains you.

Second, when you are aware of boundless space, you find that more energy is available to you. When mother and child unite—when your awareness connects with spaciousness—and as you feel more at home in that open awareness, you will naturally experience qualities that nourish you. Of course, a quality is there whether you recognize it or not, but your awareness of its presence is helpful. I am not encouraging you to *think* about a quality or to make something up, but to be *aware* of a quality. An example of merely thinking about a nourishing quality would be when you say to yourself, *I'm not supposed to feel bad; I'm supposed to feel good, so I'll think happy thoughts.* Whether you are thinking good thoughts or bad thoughts, they equally obscure openness. If you must choose between the two, good thoughts are more pleasant, but in terms of connecting with the open space of being, both good and bad thoughts are obscurations. Many psychological exercises involve generating good thoughts, but the *dzogchen* teachings do not encourage this type of practice. As the saying goes, whether you are hit on the head with a rock or with a lump of gold, the result is pain. In this teaching you are not asked to improve upon your thoughts; you are simply being aware of what is. You are not trying to "create your own reality" with thoughts, but are simply aware of the reality of joy that already exists. As you become aware of joy, that very moment is a miracle.

If you bring the awareness of joy or love to the pain identity, much of what you experience as pain is relieved. It simply dissipates. Much of what we experience as pain depends so much on how we perceive it. And the mind can also affect what we may believe to be the physical laws of the body. When you connect with unbounded space through the experiences of stillness, silence, and spaciousness, and when you experience the positive qualities that become available, you are able to host your pain without struggling. Fully hosting pain in this way frees you from the conditions in which pain arises. And during moments of awareness, every inhalation and exhalation is healing. When you bring your awareness to the simple rhythm of your breath as it moves in and out, you can experience a deep releasing and opening.

According to the teachings, the subtle underlying structures of our pain body naturally exhaust themselves as we abide in the nature of mind. We are not feeding them, so as thoughts and emotions arise, they naturally release into the openness of the mind. As they do, they no longer have the power to drive our actions. Is it possible that this exhaustion or release can affect the patterns encoded in our DNA and cells? Samsara, the endless wheel of suffering, is the result of disconnectedness from openness, the source within. When you don't recognize openness, you disconnect from yourself, and this can lead to physical illness and emotional pain. According to traditional Tibetan medicine, the source of all illness is ignorance, the failure to recognize the source of one's being. When the mother (emptiness, openness, spaciousness) and child (awareness) unite, the causes of sickness are not perpetuated. This is a traditional Tibetan way of saying that the more you are aware of openness as your mother or source, the more the momentum of the pain body's patterning is disrupted and weakened. When stress is reduced in this way, the negative consequences of that stress—your imbalanced reaction to outer difficulties—are also reduced. The ignorant, disconnected, unhealthy mind creates suffering. The moment you are aware, it changes the momentum and trajectory of your suffering. Confusion dissolves at the source.

Trusting in this process may help to encourage you to turn toward the inner refuge again and again, and that trust can also provide comfort and protection in difficult times. Yet simply trusting or believing what the teachings are saying is not enough. It is important for each of us to discover the truth of the teachings for ourselves, experientially. Apply the medicine in your life directly to the suffering you experience. You will see the proof. Be open to trusting, but take the medicine.

Imagine going to a fine restaurant and reading the menu; do you think that by reading the menu alone you are getting a nourishing meal? Of course, this sounds ridiculous. But this is, in effect, what we do in Western culture: we read a lot and think we know because we can intellectually understand what we have read, and we leave it at that, looking for the next "spin" to keep us going on the path. But this will not help free us from suffering and ignorance. Unless we engage the practice through coming to stillness, silence, and spaciousness, we are just like that person reading the menu but failing to eat. I encourage you to look deeper. Find your personal frontier of discomfort and be present there, open and aware. Host your experience fully, in open awareness. Do not disconnect from yourself by pursuing thinking or analysis. Be present. Warmly present. Be alive and awake in each moment of your life. You will be rewarded beyond the imaginations of ego.

Meditation is not just passively sitting and observing life flowing by. Rather it is an active process of engaging in transformation. Some may think you are wasting time by meditating. They would advise you to go to a movie or on a vacation rather than meditate, which looks like sitting and doing nothing. But no one else can know how much you are disconnecting from your unhealthy patterns and charging your battery by sitting and reconnecting with the source of being. Sitting down and being aware, you are changing your life. Stopping and reconnecting to the refuge of your inner being, even for a moment, you are changing your life. What you overlooked or thought was nothing becomes the deepest treasury imaginable. Perhaps like the old monk that I encountered in Tibet, you too will realize that you have everything you need to practice for the rest of your life, and in so practicing will discover the gifts available to you, sharing them with countless others you will encounter throughout your life.

AFTERWORD

Awakening the Luminous Mind completes a series of three books that present meditation instructions and practices useful to opening the three doors of body, speech, and mind, and to discovery of the treasury of the natural mind. I have found these simple practices most essential to support transformation and realization in myself and in my students. The meditation practices are the Nine Breathings of Purification and the *Tsa Lung* exercises, found in *Awakening the Sacred Body;* the Five Warrior Syllables, found in *Tibetan Sound Healing;* and now abiding in the inner refuge and the Fivefold Teaching of Dawa Gyaltsen, as presented in this book. Through learning and applying these practices, the very suffering experienced by so many through the three doors of body, speech, and mind can be recognized as opportunities for finding and connecting to our deeper, inherent wisdom. Deep healing and transformation become possible in so doing. I feel fortunate to have received these teachings, which articulate how our pain becomes a path to liberation. I continue to take these teachings to heart every day. I offer them as my gift to you. May these teachings transform your life as they have mine. May all of our endeavors result in much-needed enlightened expression and activity in our world!

Appendix

Inner Refuge

Body

The center of the victorious mandala, one's own body,
The source of all positive qualities without exception,
Is the expanse within the three channels and the five chakras.
I take refuge in this body of emptiness.

Speech

All the gathered clouds of suffering and misery
Are completely cleared by the wisdom wind,
Revealing the unelaborated, primordially pure expanse of the sky.
I take refuge in this body of light.

Mind

From the pavilion of the five wisdom lights,
Rays from nondual spheres of light emanate,
Clearing the webs of the darkness of ignorance.
I take refuge in this body of great bliss.

Dedication

All pure virtue done through the three doors,
I dedicate to the welfare of all sentient beings of the three realms.
Having purified all afflictions and obscurations of the three poisons,
May we swiftly achieve the complete buddhahood of the three bodies.

ACKNOWLEDGMENTS

Through the immeasurable generosity and kindness of my teacher, Yongdzin Sangye Tenzin Rinpoche, I received the teachings of Great Perfection, the highest vehicle among the Bön teachings. He accepted me as his student when I was a teenager, and from the beginning through completion, transmitted the core teachings of the Zhang Zhung Nyen Gyü cycle to me. The essence of those teachings are in this book. Even though he has passed away, his blessing and inspiration continue in my life.

I thank Menri Lopon Trinley Nyima, who was kindly available to look up references and discuss various points related to the dzogchen teachings presented here.

I wish to acknowledge my students throughout the world. I hold all of them dear in my heart. I particularly honor those who have loyally and consistently followed my teaching. Over time they have persisted and overcome many challenges and obstacles on the path. They continue to provide a mirror for my own journey. We have grown together. You cannot see your face unless there is a mirror; you cannot recognize your strength unless there is vulnerability, or find compassion unless there is need. By sharing their hearts with me, they have allowed me to mature as a teacher.

This is the third book that my student, Marcy Vaughn, has edited. The particular beauty of this book is a product of our evolving relationship in working together. She has assisted me in expressing the deep wisdom of these often complex teachings in a very simple, warm, accessible manner. I am grateful for her help. I envisioned these three books as the cornerstones for a program to bring practices of body, speech, and mind from my tradition to a wider audience. The Three Doors training program is the vehicle to bring these practices to those who are ready. I wish to thank Kallon Basquin, who, as the director of this emerging program, has worked tirelessly in the last couple of years. Without him, manifestation would not have been possible. I thank him for his dedication to this vision and to me personally.

I thank Patricia Gift, my editor at Hay House, for her enthusiasm for this current project and the care and advice she offered while bringing it to fruition.

Sue Davis-Dill, as the executive director of Ligmincha Institute, has assumed much responsibility in so many different areas both in the U.S. and worldwide, which has opened up space for me to expand my work and teachings. While not directly part of this book, her support gives me a necessary freedom to teach throughout the world.

My wife, Khandro Tsering Wangmo, has been generous and patient through all phases of my life and work. I am deeply grateful for her support. My son, Senghe, has helped me to grow and cultivate a warm heart. He provides unceasing opportunity to continually exercise my capacity to maintain warmth through stillness, silence, and spaciousness!

About the Author

Tenzin Wangyal Rinpoche is an acclaimed author and teacher of students around the world. He is highly respected for his depth of wisdom, his engaging teaching style, and his ability to make ancient Tibetan teachings clear, accessible, and relevant to the lives of Westerners. Tenzin Rinpoche is the founder and spiritual director of Ligmincha Institute, a nonprofit organization in Shipman, Virginia, dedicated to preserving the ancient teachings, arts, sciences, language, and literature of Tibet and Zhang Zhung, the ancient kingdom associated with the Bön tradition. He is the author of *Tibetan Yogas of Body, Speech, and Mind; Awakening the Sacred Body; Tibetan Sound Healing; The Tibetan Yogas of Dream and Sleep; Healing with Form, Energy, and Light; Wonders of the Natural Mind;* and *Unbounded Wholeness* (with Anne Klein). Tenzin Rinpoche resides in California with his wife and son. For more information about Tenzin Rinpoche's activities, please visit www.ligmincha.org.

Tenzin Rinpoche has created a secular educational organization called Three Doors: Transformations of Body, Speech, and Mind, in order to offer instruction in the teachings described in this book, through workshops and retreats. It is hoped that these simple and profound practices will make their way into prisons and hospitals, boardrooms and think tanks, classrooms and studios, and that they will transcend barriers of culture and belief to support many who could benefit from their potent medicine. Please visit the website for more information and to participate in this venture, if you are moved to do so at: www.the3doors.org.

PRACTICE NOTES

PRACTICE NOTES

PRACTICE NOTES

Practice Notes

Practice Notes

PRACTICE NOTES

PRACTICE NOTES

Practice Notes

PRACTICE NOTES

PRACTICE NOTES

PRACTICE NOTES

PRACTICE NOTES

PRACTICE NOTES

Hay House Titles of Related Interest

YOU CAN HEAL YOUR LIFE, *the movie,*
starring Louise L. Hay & Friends
(available as a 1-DVD program and an expanded 2-DVD set)
Watch the trailer at: **www.LouiseHayMovie.com**

THE SHIFT, *the movie,*
starring Dr. Wayne W. Dyer
(available as a 1-DVD program and an expanded 2-DVD set)
Watch the trailer at: **www.DyerMovie.com**

≈ ≈ ≈

*THE END OF SUFFERING AND THE DISCOVERY OF
HAPPINESS: The Path of Tibetan Buddhism,*
by His Holiness the Dalai Lama

*THE MINDFUL MANIFESTO: How Doing Less and Noticing
More Can Help Us Thrive in a Stressed-Out World,*
by Dr. Jonty Heaversedge and Ed Halliwell

*A MINDFUL NATION: How a Simple Practice Can
Help Us Reduce Stress, Improve Performance,
and Recapture the American Spirit,*
by Congressman Tim Ryan

WHY MEDITATE?: Working with Thoughts and Emotions,
by Matthieu Ricard

All of the above are available at your local bookstore,
or may be ordered by contacting Hay House (see next page).

≈ ≈ ≈

We hope you enjoyed this Hay House book.
If you'd like to receive our online catalog featuring
additional information on Hay House books and
products, or if you'd like to find out more about the
Hay Foundation, please contact:

Hay House, Inc., P.O. Box 5100, Carlsbad, CA 92018-5100
(760) 431-7695 or (800) 654-5126
(760) 431-6948 (fax) or (800) 650-5115 (fax)
www.hayhouse.com® • **www.hayfoundation.org**

≈ ≈ ≈

Published and distributed in Australia by:
Hay House Australia Pty. Ltd., 18/36 Ralph St., Alexandria NSW 2015
Phone: 612-9669-4299 • *Fax:* 612-9669-4144 • www.hayhouse.com.au

Published and distributed in the United Kingdom by:
Hay House UK, Ltd., 292B Kensal Rd., London W10 5BE • *Phone:*
44-20-8962-1230 • *Fax:* 44-20-8962-1239 • www.hayhouse.co.uk

Published and distributed in the Republic of South Africa by:
Hay House SA (Pty), Ltd., P.O. Box 990, Witkoppen 2068
Phone/Fax: 27-11-467-8904 • www.hayhouse.co.za

Published in India by: Hay House Publishers India, Muskaan
Complex, Plot No. 3, B-2, Vasant Kunj, New Delhi 110 070 • *Phone:*
91-11-4176-1620 • *Fax:* 91-11-4176-1630 • www.hayhouse.co.in

Distributed in Canada by:
Raincoast, 9050 Shaughnessy St., Vancouver, B.C. V6P 6E5 •
Phone: (604) 323-7100 • *Fax:* (604) 323-2600 • www.raincoast.com

Take Your Soul on a Vacation

Visit **www.HealYourLife.com®** to regroup, recharge,
and reconnect with your own magnificence.
Featuring blogs, mind-body-spirit news, and life-changing
wisdom from Louise Hay and friends.

Visit **www.HealYourLife.com** today!